MALAYA
500 Early Postcards

First published in 2008 by
EDITIONS DIDIER MILLET
35B Boat Quay
Singapore 049824

Reprinted in 2015

www.edmbooks.com

Editorial Director
TIMOTHY AUGER

Editor
GREGORY LEE

Designer
NELANI JINADASA

Production Manager
SIN KAM CHEONG

Colour Separation by
COLOURSCAN CO PTE LTD,
SC GRAPHIC TECHNOLOGY PTE LTD

Printed by
TWP SDN. BHD., MALAYSIA

ISBN 978-981-4155-98-4

Front cover: CLOCK TOWER, F.M.S. RAILWAYS, PENANG (c 1930)
Divided-back
Publisher: Unknown

Back cover: CHINESE PERANAKAN LADY (c 1930)
Divided-back
Publisher: Unknown

MALAYA
500 Early Postcards

Cheah Jin Seng

EDITIONS DIDIER MILLET

Johore Hotel, Johore.

CONTENTS

View Album of Johore

UNFEDERATED MALAY STATE

A SERIES OF EXCLUSIVE VIEWS
PRINTED IN REAL PHOTOGRAVURE

AN OVERVIEW

The inspiration for this book comes from two books published earlier by Editions Didier Millet: *Indonesia: 500 Early Postcards* by Leo Haks and Steven Wachlin (2004),[1] and *Singapore: 500 Early Postcards* (2006).[2]

For most of the period covered by this book, Malaya (sometimes known as "British Malaya") comprised the Straits Settlements (SS), made up of Singapore, Malacca, Penang, Province Wellesley, the Dindings, Labuan, Christmas Island and the Cocos Islands; the Federated Malay States (FMS), made up of Perak, Selangor, Negri Sembilan and Pahang; and the Unfederated Malay States (UMS), consisting of Johore, Kedah, Perlis, Kelantan and Trengganu.[3] Taken together, these entities occupied essentially what is known to geographers as the "Malay Peninsula". This publication will cover the Federated Malay States; the Unfederated Malay States; and Malacca and Penang.

Picture postcards (ppcs) of Malaya have been featured in four books published by Major David Ng. They are: *Malaya/A Retrospect of the Country through Postcards* (1983);[4] *Penang/The City and Suburbs in the Early 20th Century* (1986);[5] *Kuala Lumpur in Postcards, 1900–1930* (1987);[6] and *Malaya-Lifestyles/1900–1930* (1989).[7] In 1986, more than 500 ppcs of Penang were illustrated in *Penang/Through Old Picture Postcards,*[8] published by the Penang Museum. Slightly more, 650 ppcs, were featured in the comprehensive *Penang Postcards Collection: 1899-1930s* by Khoo Salma Nasution and Malcolm Wade (2003).[9] *Reminiscences of the Straits Settlements through Postcards* (2005)[10] showcased ppcs of Singapore, Malacca and Penang, and was based on a series of joint exhibitions mounted by the National Archives of Malaysia and Singapore.

The most commonly found ppcs of Malaya are those of Penang before the Second World War. In contrast, not a single ppc of prewar Perlis is known to this author. Ppcs from Perak, Selangor, Johore, Malacca and Negri Sembilan are far less common than those of Penang, while ppcs of Pahang, Kedah, Kelantan and Trengganu are scarce.

This book is arranged on a geographical basis, and the main galleries are complemented by an additional chapter on ppc booklets, multiviews and panoramic ppcs. Various philatelic aspects of ppcs are also discussed.

Above: PENANG. NATIVE MARKET.
Back: Divided
Publisher: Raphael Tuck & Sons

Opposite: *The front cover of a Johore photographic views booklet entitled "View Album of Johore/Unfederated Malay State".*
Publisher: F.J. Treusein, Johore Bahru
The waterfront of Johore Bahru around 1920.

EARLY HISTORY of PICTURE POSTCARDS of MALAYA

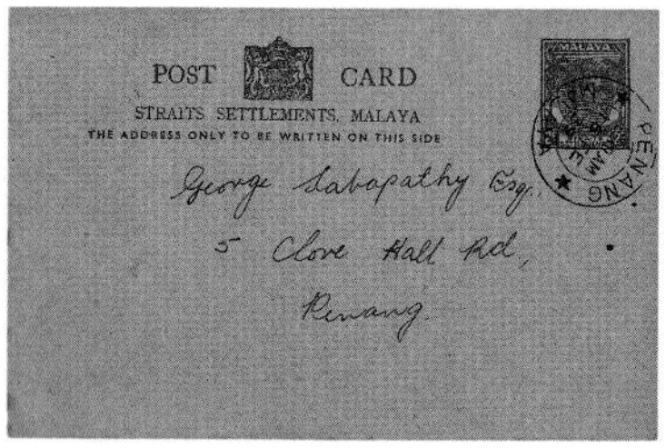

The addressee's mailing address was usually written on the front of the pspc.

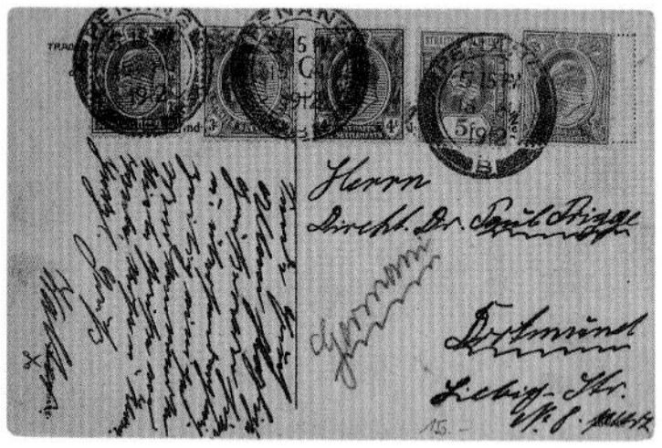

The reverse side of this ppc shows that it was sent from Penang to Germany in 1912.

Origin of the picture postcard

The earliest known of any postcards are the private cards, known as the "Lipman's Postal Cards", that were printed in the United States in 1861. Austria is credited with the production of the first official (governmental) postcard in 1869, following a proposal put forward by Dr Heinrich von Stephan, the director of its postal service, in 1865. The Straits Settlements (SS) (comprising Singapore, Malacca and Penang) introduced the first postcard in 1879.

A distinction can in fact be made between two types of postcard (pc): the postal stationery postcard (pspc) (*upper left*) and the picture postcard (ppc) (*lower left*). The first picture postcard (ppc) was produced in Britain in 1894. By the end of the 19th century, picture postcards (ppcs) were produced almost worldwide.

The Straits Settlements

Captain Francis Light founded Penang for the British in 1786. Sir Stamford Raffles established Singapore in 1819, while Malacca came under British rule in 1824 under the terms of the so-called Anglo-Dutch Treaty. These were the principle components of the Straits Settlements (SS). During its early years, the SS was administered from India (the Fourth Presidency of the East India Company in 1826, the Bengal Presidency in 1830, the British Indian Government in 1858). From 1 April 1867 onwards the SS was a British Crown Colony. The first Governor of the Straits Settlements was Sir Harry St George Ord; he was based in Singapore.[10, 16]

As part of the Straits Settlements, Singapore and Penang developed much faster than Malacca due to their geographical position, free port status, patterns of trade, and rapid migration. Hence, many more travellers have visited Singapore and Penang than Malacca; this explains why there are many more ppcs of Singapore and Penang than of Malacca. Pangkor Island and the Dindings (Perak) were also part of the SS for a time (1826–1935), as were Christmas Island and Cocos Island (1886–1955), while Labuan in Borneo was administered by the SS from 1907 to 1941.[64]

The Federated Malay States

The Federated Malay States (FMS) consisted of Selangor, Perak, Negri Sembilan and Pahang. The FMS was officially established on 1 July 1896. It might be considered a first step in the direction of the present federal government system of Malaysia. The FMS was formed after the British intervened in the administration of Pahang in 1888. Kuala Lumpur became the FMS capital. Sir Frank Swettenham was the first Resident-General (1896–1900); the first High Commissioner was Sir Charles Mitchell (1896–1899) who was simultaneously the Governor of the Straits Settlements. The Resident-General was based in Kuala Lumpur[12] while the High Commissioner was based in Singapore.

The Unfederated Malay States

The Unfederated Malay States (UMS) consisted of Perlis, Kedah, Kelantan, Trengganu and Johore. Under the terms of the Anglo-Siamese Treaty of 1909, Britain gained control of Perlis, Kedah, Kelantan and Trengganu from the Siamese. British Advisers were appointed to Perlis,

Kedah and Kelantan in 1909, and Trengganu in 1918. Johore did not have a British Adviser until 1914. In the UMS, the Malays enjoyed greater autonomy than in the FMS; the administrative machinery was largely in the hands of the Malays.[12] The FMS and UMS disappeared as political entities when the Federation of Malaya was formed in 1948.

Early picture postcards of Malaya

In view of the colonial history shared by these two countries, it is not surprising that the history of ppcs in Malaya in general is similar to that in Singapore.

The earliest known ppc of Malaya (Penang) was dated 1 August 1898 [1]; this is a year earlier than the earliest card described by Khoo and Wade. This type of card may be described as a ppc with multiple vignettes or thumbnail views, or as a photomontage.[9] Another early ppc of Penang [2] was sent on 10 December 1898 to Austria. Ppcs of Malaya prior to 1900 are rare. One other rare example [3] in the author's collection is a black-and-white multiview ppc also sent from Penang to Austria.

The earliest ppcs in 1897 consisted of the 3¢ carmine Queen Victoria postal stationery postcard (pspc) issued in 1893 by the postal department of the Straits Settlements. A thin black-and-white real photograph or picture was layered on the message side; the result is known as a postal stationery ppc (psppc).[2] [4 (*next page, upper left*)] shows a private home-made psppc of a photograph of a European man and his two children (5.5 x 7.5 cm or 2.6 x 2.9 inches) glued on the message side of a FMS pspc; [5 (*next page, lower left*); 6] show two privately drawn and painted ppcs sent in 1899 to England from Bidor (near Telok Anson), Perak.

Undivided and divided backs, and postal rates

Under the Universal Postal Union (UPU) regulations, the address side of the postcard was reserved for the sticking of the postage stamp, the writing of the name of the addressee and the destination address. This "Undivided-Back" ppc format (*upper right*) has no central vertical line. The obverse side (picture or view side) has either one picture or multiple vignettes occupying a portion, with the remaining empty space reserved for the message.

Prior to 1906, ppcs in Malaya were Undivided-Backs. As in Singapore, the "Divided-Back" format was introduced in 1906.[2] Divided-Back ppcs (*lower right*) had a vertical line separating the name and address of the addressee from the message, thus permitting a longer message to be written. This was an obvious advantage over Undivided-Back ppcs although the latter continued to be sold and used after 1906, as publishers had considerable stocks of them.[2]

Postal rates varied according to the destination and period. For local addresses within the SS and FMS the rate started at 1¢ in 1899, and rose to 4¢ by 1941. The British Empire rate started at 3¢ and rose to 4¢, with the postal rates for the rest of the world moving from 3¢ to 8¢ during over the same period. The 3¢ rate was the most common rate for British colonies.

During the early years, using the "printed matter" rate was a cheap way to send ppcs. Hence a lot of ppcs exist with the word "POSTCARD" deleted and replaced by other terms such as "PRINTED MATTER", "PRINTED PAPER" or even "BOOK POST".

With the advent of regular air services in the 1930s special airmail rates for ppcs were introduced. However, these rates were much more expensive than printed matter rates, and were not often used.

The period 1906–1914 might be considered the "Golden Era of Picture Postcards" with a rise in the number of cheap privately printed ppcs, and postal rates. It ended with the outbreak of the First World War.[2]

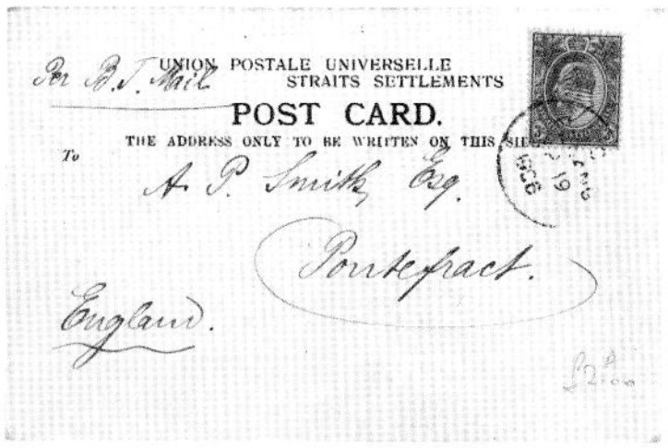

This Undivided-Back ppc was sent from Penang to England in 1906.

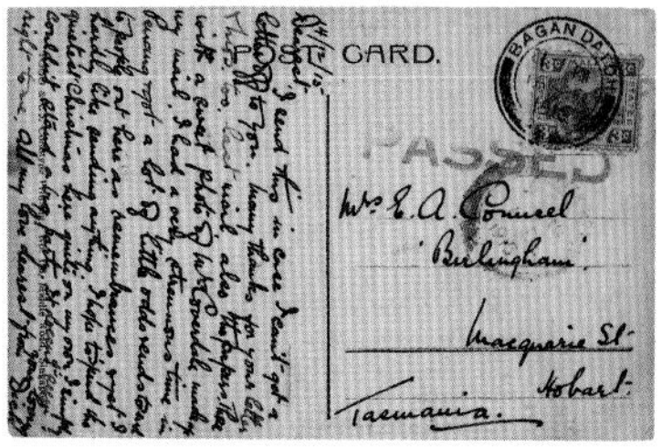

This ppc was sent in 1915 from Perak to Tasmania. The word "PASSED" stamped at the top right corner indicates that it was censored.

Some postcards were home-made. In this particular case, a picture was glued onto the front!
(*See* [4])

Another example of a home-made ppc: an image of a lion wearing a crown is beautifully drawn and coloured.
(*See* [5])

A portrait photograph of G.R. Lambert.

The colour of the picture

Most early ppcs of Malaya are in black-and-white (especially the photographic ppcs) or in multicolour. Though monochrome ppcs in Singapore exist in sepia, azure, green or orange colours, only black-and-white and sepia-toned ppcs have been found in Malaya.

The photographers

The ppc is a product of photography, and its history parallels advances in photographic technology. Most of the early publishers of ppcs in Malaya were German photographers.

The first ppcs of Singapore were published by the German photographer G.R. Lambert (*bottom left*),[2] who also published ppcs of Malaya (Johore, Pahang, Malacca and Perak). However, in Penang, the first ppcs were produced by another German photographer, August Kaulfuss, who did not produce any Singapore ppcs.[9, 11] Perhaps the two German photographers had demarcated their territories!

G.R. Lambert opened his photographic studio in 1875, but he left Singapore in 1885 and, from 1885 to 1905, the firm was managed by another German, Alexander Koch. From 1905, the firm was managed by H.T. Jansen, also German.[2] Their head office was in Singapore, but they had a branch in Kuala Lumpur as well.[16] It was in this branch that many ppcs of Johore, Kuala Lumpur and Perak were produced.

August Kaulfuss was the oldest and most established European photographer in Penang. He was born in 1861 and came to Penang in 1883, before starting up his photography business three years later. He produced many photographs of locations from Penang to Johore. He was also photographer to the Sultan of Kedah.[16] Kaulfuss published many beautiful ppcs of Penang and northern Malaya. C.J. Kleingrothe, another German photographer based in Medan, Dutch East Indies, published a few ppcs of Penang during the early 1900s.[9]

The Japanese photographer/publisher M.S. Nakajima (see below) was truly pan-Malayan – he published ppcs of Penang and most of the other Malayan states, and of Singapore.[2]

The publishers

Ppc publishers are often given as the photographers of the ppcs; often no distinction can be made between the two roles, so far as the imprint on the ppc is concerned.

Besides G.R. Lambert and August Kaulfuss, mentioned above, two other publishers are known to have produced ppcs of the whole of Malaya and Singapore. They are Raphael Tuck & Sons of London, and Nakajima & Co. of Singapore.

Raphael Tuck & Sons had been established in London in 1806 and the firm was the "Art Publishers to the King and Queen". They produced numerous multicolour "Oilette" ppcs of the "Wide Wide World"; these included several of Penang, Kuala Lumpur and Singapore.

Nakajima & Co., a firm based in Singapore, were artistic photographers who produced many photographic ppcs of Penang, Malaya and Singapore. Rumour has it that they were spies for Japan prior to its invasion of Malaya and Singapore in 1941–2, for among their favourite subjects were strategic infrastructure such as bridges, roads, railways, rubber plantations and ports.

Koh & Co. published a few beautiful ppcs of Johore and Malaya. The firm was founded in Singapore by Mr Koh Hoon Teck in 1905. According to its advertisement in 1908, the price of uncoloured ppcs was 30¢ per dozen; those of colured ones were 50¢ per dozen. (The price of Tuck's ppcs was $1.20 per dozen.[2])

Other publishers did exist, such as The Federal Rubber Stamp Co., S.M. Manicum, M.J. Penang etc., but little is known about them.

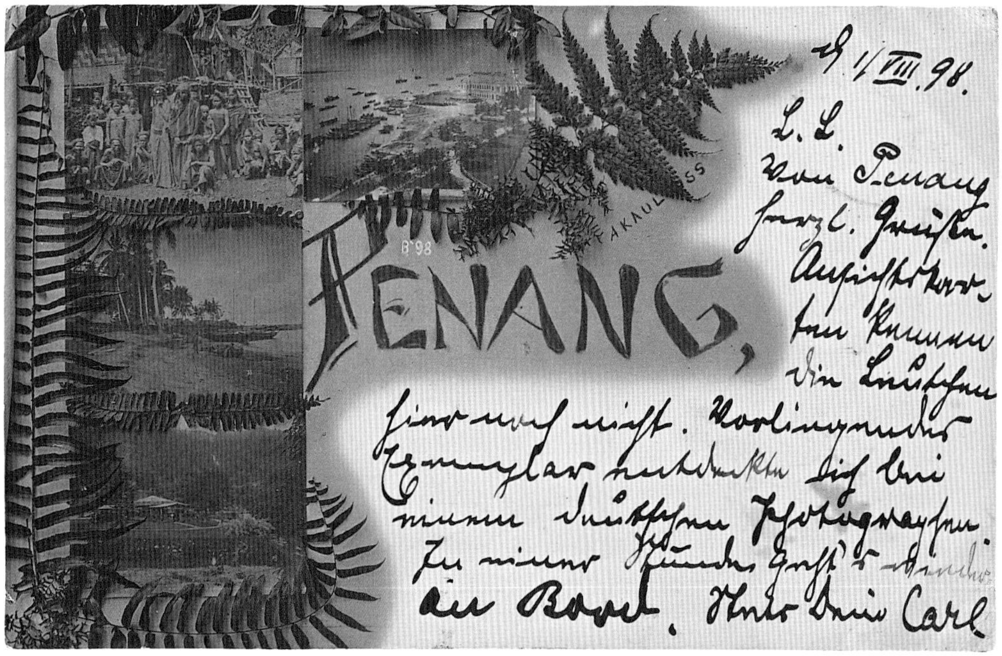

[1]
PENANG.

Cancellation: 1898
Back: Undivided
Publisher: A. Kaulfuss, Penang

The earliest postcard in the author's collection, this is a black-and-white photographic ppc with multiple views of Penang (waterfall garden, Tanjong Bungah beach, a group of Indians and Swettenham Pier).

[2]
PINANG.

Cancellation: 1898
Back: Undivided
Publisher: A. Kaulfuss, Penang

An early photographic ppc sent from Penang to Austria on 10 December 1898, it is in a light sepia tone and has two photographic views of Penang (a group of Malays and the Waterfall Garden, and the Botanic Gardens).

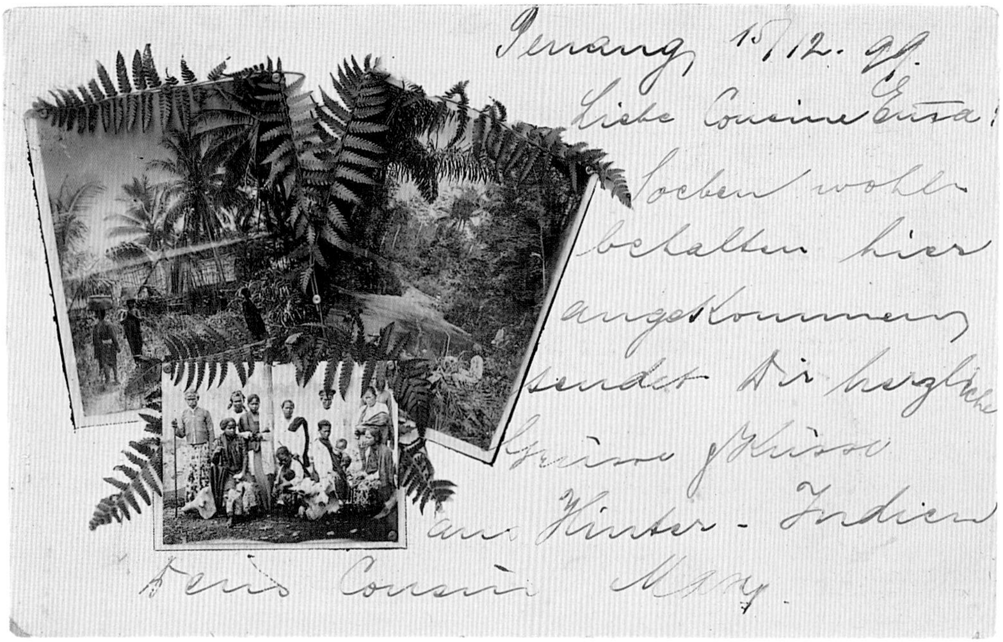

[3]
Untitled.

Cancellation: 1899
Back: Undivided
Publisher: Not stated but attributed to A. Kaulfuss, Penang

A multiview black-and-white photographic ppc sent from Penang to Austria on 15 December 1899.

[4]
Untitled.

Cancellation: 1901
Back: Undivided

A private home-made postcard with a photograph of a European man and his two children. The photograph is glued to the postcard.

[5]
Untitled.

Cancellation: 1899
Back: Undivided

A home-made postcard with a picture of a lion wearing a crown. The postcard was sent from Bidor, Perak, to England in 1899.

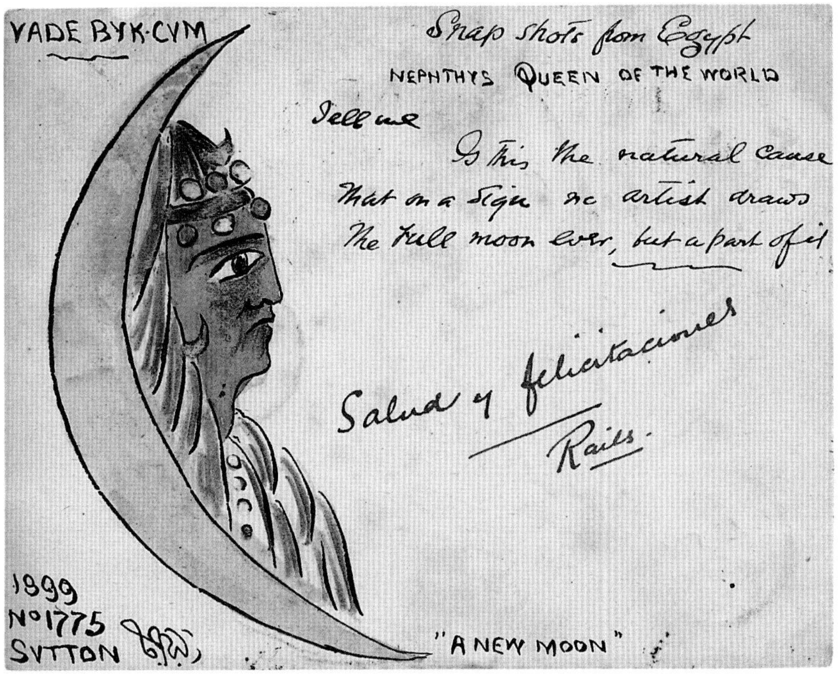

[6]
"A New Moon".

Cancellation: 1899
Back: Undivided

This postcard consists of a home-drawn and coloured picture showing "Nephthys Queen of the World". It probably came from the same source as [5], as it was also sent from Bidor.

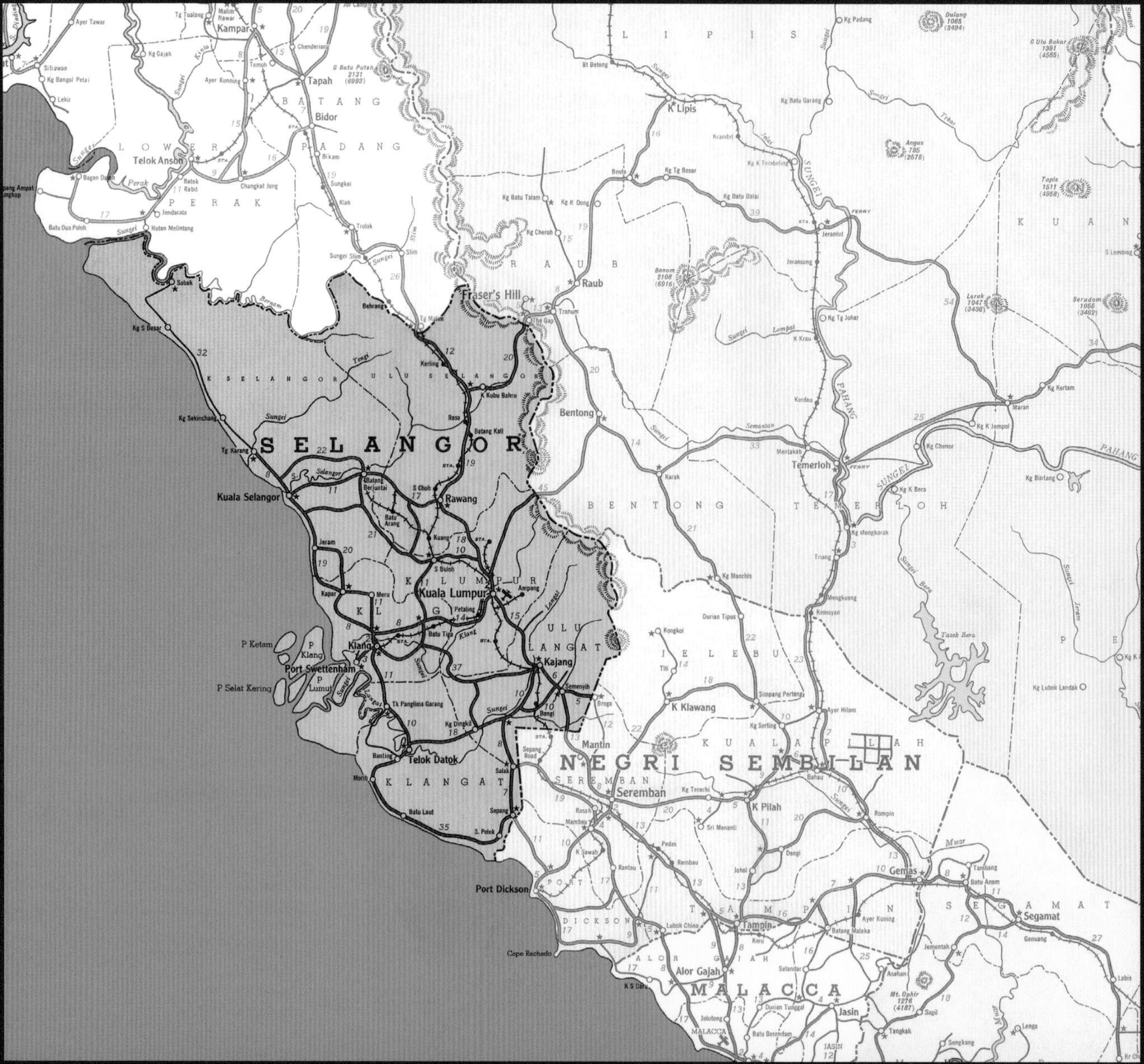

SELANGOR
NEGRI SEMBILAN
MALACCA
LIPIS
RAUB
BENTONG
TEMERLOH
JELEBU
KUALA PILAH
SEREMBAN
PORT DICKSON
TAMPIN
ALOR GAJAH
SEGAMAT
KLANGAT
ULU LANGAT
ULU SELANGOR
K SELANGOR
KUALA LUMPUR
KLANG
BATANG PADANG
LOWER PERAK
PAHANG
Kampar
Tapah
Bidor
Telok Anson
Sabak
Fraser's Hill
Raub
K Lipis
Bentong
Karak
Temerloh
Jerantut
Maran
Rawang
Kuala Selangor
Tg Karang
Kuala Lumpur
Ampang
Klang
Port Swettenham
P Ketam
P Klang
P Selat Kering
Kajang
Semenyih
Telok Datok
Banting
Batu Laut
Sepang
Mantin
Seremban
K Pilah
K Klawang
Rembau
Port Dickson
Cape Rachado
Gemas
Tampin
Alor Gajah
Jasin
Segamat
Tasek Bera
Mt. Ophir 1276 (4187)
Benom 2108 (6916)
Sungei Pahang

SELANGOR

The establishment on 1 July 1896 of the Federated Malay States (FMS), comprising the four states of Selangor, Perak, Negri Sembilan and Pahang, can be seen in retrospect as the first step towards the present federal government system of Malaysia. The formation of the FMS was the consequence of the problems (in-fighting between the various Malay groups) the British faced after intervening in the administration of Pahang. Heading the federation was a Resident-General based at Kuala Lumpur, the capital of Selangor, which later became the federal capital because of its central position.[12]

Selangor lies on the west coast of the Malay Peninsula. The name Selangor, is said to have originated from the Malay word *selangau*, or "fly"; this was probably due to the abundance of flies in the marshes along the Selangor River. Another theory suggests that the name was derived from the term *Selang Ur* ("land of the straits"). Selangor is also known by its Arabic honorific, Darul Ehsan ("Abode of Sincerity").

In the 15th century Selangor was ruled by Malacca. After the fall of Malacca to the Portuguese in 1511, the area was hotly disputed by Portugal, Johore, Acheh and Siam. However, it was Bugis mercenaries who eventually established the current Sultanate in 1766. In the 19th century, Selangor's economy boomed due to the exploitation of huge tin reserves and the growing importance of rubber. Today, Selangor is the richest and most urbanised of all the Malay states.

The Sultans of Selangor

The constitutional head of Selangor is the Sultan, whose role is largely ceremonial; the position is hereditary. Sultan Sir Alaeddin Sulaiman Shah [7] ruled from 1898 to 1938. Indian bodyguards of the Sultan (and Governor of the Straits Settlements and Visiting Royalty) are shown in [8]. The Sultan lived in Klang; his old Istana is shown in [9] while the new Istana is shown in [10 (*upper right*)]. In 1903, a conference (Durbar) of the Sultans of Malaya was held in Kuala Lumpur; an impressive Conference Hall was built in the vicinity of the Lake Gardens [11].

Carcosa

In prewar Selangor, the Sultan was the constitutional head, with political power residing in the hands of the Selangor British Resident and the Resident-General of the FMS. "Carcosa" was the official residence of the Resident-General; it was built in 1898 on a hillock overlooking the Lake Gardens. Sir Frank Swettenham, the first Resident-General, lived in Carcosa from 1898 to 1901;[14,15] indeed, it was he who coined its name inspired by a book entitled the *The King In Yellow* by R. Chambers.[15] He said: "I did not call it Government or King's House because neither seemed an appropriate name in the Protected States. I did not give it a Malay name because it was to be the residence of a British Officer... I imagine[d] it [to be] the Castle of the King in yellow..."[14] Carcosa [13] has more recently been redeveloped into a luxurious hotel, the "Carcosa Seri Negara".[15]

Sir Frank built another mansion ("The Residency" [14]) as the official home of the British Resident of Selangor. When the Prince of Wales visited Kuala Lumpur in 1922 [12], he stayed at The Residency; it was later the official residence and office of the first Prime Minister of Malaysia, Tunku Abdul Rahman.

Hospitals and health

In 1906, there were eight hospitals at Kuala Lumpur, which included the European Hospital [15; 16], Pauper Hospital [17; 18 (*lower right*)] and Tung Shin Yi Yuen (Chinese

The façade of the Sultan's new palace had impressive Islamic domes and minarets. (*See* [10])

This is likely to be the "free" ward in the Government General Hospital. (*See* [18])

The Kuala Lumpur Railway Station was a major railway hub for the Federated Malay States. (*See* [24])

The Bangunan Sultan Abdul Samad took its name from the reigning sultan of Selangor. (*See* [33])

Hospital) [19].[16] The Institute for Medical Research (IMR) [20] was established at the instigation of Sir Frank Swettenham in 1900; the IMR pioneered medical research and outstanding advances were made in combating diseases such as malaria, beri-beri and filariasis.[17]

Founding of Kuala Lumpur

Kuala Lumpur (KL), the federal capital of Malaysia, is the main gateway to the country. Its name means "muddy river mouth", reflecting the city's humble origins as a malaria-plagued tin-mining community. At the confluence of the Klang and the Gombak Rivers stands the Masjid Jamek [21]; it was the first large mosque to be built in KL; it was designed by a Government architect A.B. Hubback and declared open in 1909.[15]

The Railway Station

As KL is an inland city, many visitors during the prewar era travelled to KL by train. The Railway Station (1911) [22-24; 26] along Jalan Sultan Hishamuddin is one of the most notable landmarks in KL, with a distinctive architectural style. Designed by A.B. Hubback in a British "Raj" style, sometimes known as the "Mogul" style, the station was once described by a traveller in the 1930s as being "of the late Marzipan period".[19] Like all major railway stations in Malaya, the KL Railway Station incorporated a hotel [25] within its premises.

Opposite the station was the Malaya Railway Administration Building [27; 28]. It was also designed by Hubback and completed in 1917. The Empire Hotel [29] and the Majestic Hotel [30] were nearby.

Bangunan Sultan Abdul Samad

This building was named after Selangor's Sultan Abdul Samad, who reigned from 1857 to 1898. It was completed in 1897. Today, the gleaming copper domes, the 40-metre clock tower and stately arched colonnades of the Bangunan Sultan Abdul Samad stretch just as majestically along Jalan Raja as they did more than a century ago. This irrepressible building is one of the most impressive landmarks in KL.[19]

The architects of the Bangunan Sultan Abdul Samad were Charles Norman, who designed the ground plan of the building in a "Mahometan" style, and R.A.J. Bidwell, who completed it. The building is two storeys high; the symmetrical façade is punctuated by two towers, one on each side of the central clock tower. All three towers have onion-shaped domes with copper coverings [31; 33 (*lower left*)]. This building is one of the most photographed in prewar KL. It also set a new trend for civic buildings; several other buildings in similarly grand style were built within its vicinity [32-36].

The Selangor Club

The Padang (now known as Dataran Merdeka) lies between the Bangunan Sultan Abdul Samad and the Selangor Club [37; 38]. At its corner lay another icon of the colonial era – the Cops Fountain [38]; it was built in 1897 in memory of Steve Harper, an inspector from the Selangor Military Police. The Selangor Club is a Mock-Tudor-style building completed in 1890. Its nickname is "The Spotted Dog", due in part to a clumsy rendition of its first emblem, a leopard.[15]

Near the Selangor Club and the Padang are two other historic buildings: the former Chartered Bank of India, Australia and China (predecessor of Standard Chartered Bank) was built in 1891 [39; 40] – the building now houses the National History Museum; and St Mary's Church [41; 42], built in 1895 and now St Mary's Cathedral. St Mary's, representing the Church of England, was not only a place of worship but also a weekend social centre for the colonial community.[15]

The Lake Club and Gardens

The Lake Club [43-45] is in the Lake Gardens beside Jalan

Parliament. It was founded in 1890, and its history is interlinked with that of the Selangor Club; disgruntled members from the Selangor Club established the Lake Club. The Golf Club, another club with its roots in prewar KL, is shown in [46]. The Lake Gardens (now called Taman Tasik Perdana) [47; 48] were opened on 13 May 1889, owing much to the hard work of Alfred Venning, the State Treasurer of Selangor, and the support of Sir Frank Swettenham, the Resident.[15] Near the Lake Gardens was the Selangor Museum [49; 50], the forerunner of Muzium Negara (National Museum).

Kapitan Yap Kwan Seng

Yap Ah Loy (1837–1885) was the third Kapitan Cina of Kuala Lumpur while Yap Kwan Seng (1846–1901) was the last; the post was abolished upon his death. Yap Kwan Seng had left China aged 18, settling initially in Seremban and later in KL after he had become a very rich tin miner; at one point in time, he had 7,000 employees! [51] shows his garden house in KL; he and his fellow Hakkas built a Hakka Kongsi [53] in Sultan Street.

Roads, streets and other places of interest

Along Brickfields Road in KL were a temple and a Catholic church [52; 54]. The ppcs [55–58] show Ampang Road and the Race Course, while [59–66] show various other roads and streets. Schools in KL are depicted in [67–71]; the Slaughter House (abattoir) and the Federal Home for Women and Girls are shown in [72; 73].

Discovered in 1878 by the famous biologist, William Hornaday, the Batu Caves [74] lie 13 kilometres north of KL in Selayang. In 1891, the Indian Community built the Sri Subramaniamswamy Temple there.[15] Now more than a million devotees and tourists flock to visit the caves every year. Ppcs [75–80] show other places of interest in Selangor.

Klang and Port Swettenham (Port Klang)

Klang (or Kelang) is located 32 kilometres to the west of KL and 6 kilometres east of Port Klang. Klang was the royal capital of Selangor before the emergence of KL. After KL became a federal territory, a new capital was established at Shah Alam. Klang probably derived its name from the Klang River, which runs through the town. Various views of the town in the 1900s are shown in [81–86].

Port Klang was originally known as Port Swettenham [87–92]. The port was declared open in 1901; its development was rapid due to the extension of a railway line from KL to the port. Today, Port Klang is one of the main ports of Malaysia.

Rubber and tin

Rubber and tin brought great wealth and prosperity to Selangor. In 1876, the British had imported rubber seeds to Ceylon and Singapore from Brazil. This initiative paid off handsomely. In the 1900s, the price of rubber rose rapidly due to the growth of the motor vehicle industry. As a result, rubber estates and related industries expanded throughout Malaya. The large estates were owned mainly by the British [94] and by wealthy Chinese planters; many Indian migrants [93] came to work there.

However, Malaya's most consistent export during the 19th century was tin. Demand for tin increased sharply due to the expansion of food canning in Europe and America. The tin-mining industry had initially been dominated by the Malays, but by the late 19th century, mining on a large scale was being undertaken by both the Chinese and the Europeans [95–97].[12]

Land of the tiger

Up to the 19th century, tigers [98] roamed freely in the jungles of Selangor. However, the advent of the rubber and tin-mining industries resulted in the clearing of large areas of jungle. This, coupled with indiscriminate wildlife hunting, led to their virtual extinction.

The dome of the clock tower of the Bangunan Sultan Abdul Samad can be seen in the background.
(*See* [60])

Now called Medan Pasar, Old Market Square was a gambling centre in Kuala Lumpur during the early 20th century.
(*See* [64])

[7]
H.H. THE SULTAN OF SELANGOR AND SUITE.

Cancellation: Nil
Back: Divided
Publisher: G.R. Lambert & Co. Ltd, Singapore

Sultan Sir Alaeddin Sulaiman Shah (1898–1938) is seated in the centre; he is surrounded by his aides. Date: c 1910

[8]
INDIAN BODY GUARDS, KUALA LUMPUR.

Cancellation: 1910
Back: Divided
Publisher: G.R. Lambert & Co. Ltd, Singapore

Indian (Sikh) Body Guards bearing ceremonial lances on horseback are lined up for inspection.

[9]
OLD ISTANA OF SULTAN OF SELANGOR, KLANG.

Cancellation: Nil
Back: Divided
Series and/or No.: 90
Publisher: The Federal Rubber Stamp Co., Kuala Lumpur

The old Istana, shown here c 1906, was a relatively modest building compared to its successor.

[10]
SULTAN'S PALACE. KLANG.

Cancellation: 1925
Back: Divided

Istana Mahkota, Sultan Alaeddin Sulaiman's new palace, had impressive Islamic domes and minarets.

[11]

NATIVE CHIEFS' CONFERENCE HALL, PUBLIC GARDENS, KUALA LUMPUR, JULY 1908.

Cancellation: 1909
Back: Divided
Series and/or No.: 15
Publisher: The Federal Rubber Stamp Co., Kuala Lumpur

This building was constructed for the second Malayan Durbar (meeting of Malay rulers and British officials) held in Kuala Lumpur in July 1903.

[12]

H.R.H. PRINCE OF WALES' EASTERN TOUR, (FEDERATED MALAY STATES).

Cancellation: Nil
Back: Divided
Series and/or No.: G. Beagles' Postcards, 321
Publisher: Central News Ltd

During his visit to Kuala Lumpur in 1922, the Prince of Wales was greeted at the Padang by a large gathering of schoolchildren.

[13]
Kuala Lumpur—"Carcosa" (Government House).

Cancellation: 1905
Back: Divided
Series and/or No.: 29
Publisher: J. Brignon

Carcosa, the official residence of the Resident-General of the FMS, is now a luxury hotel.

[14]
Kuala Lumpur – The Residency.

Cancellation: Nil
Back: Undivided
Publisher: G.R. Lambert & Co. Ltd, Singapore

The Residency was built in 1899 as the official residence of the British Resident of Selangor.

[15]
EUROPEAN HOSPITAL, KUALA LUMPUR.

Cancellation: 1914
Back: Divided
Series and/or No.: 191
Publisher: The Federal Rubber Stamp Co., Kuala Lumpur

The hospital is perched on top of a small hill. Date: c 1910

[16]
THE EUROPEAN HOSPITAL, KUALA LUMPUR, F.M.S.

Cancellation: Nil
Back: Divided
Series and/or No.: M59
Publisher: M.S. Nakajima, Kuala Lumpur

A photographic close-up view of the hospital in black-and-white. Date: c 1910

[17]
PAUPER HOSPITAL, KUALA LUMPUR.

Cancellation: 1909
Back: Divided
Series and/or No.: 36
Publisher: The Federal Rubber Stamp Co., Kuala Lumpur

This is the entrance to the Government General Hospital.

[18]
VAGRANT WARD, KUALA LUMPUR.

Cancellation: 1919
Back: Divided
Series and/or No.: 27
Publisher: The Federal Rubber Stamp Co., Kuala Lumpur

This is likely to be the "free" ward in the Government General Hospital. The ppc was sent from Ipoh to Algeria (an uncommon destination).

[19]
"Tung Shin Yi Yuen" (Chinese Hospital), Kuala Lumpur.

Cancellation: Nil
Back: Divided
Series and/or No.: 43
Publisher: The Federal Rubber Stamp Co., Kuala Lumpur

This hospital, the forerunner of the present "Tong Shin" Maternity Hospital, was established in 1892 by Kapitan China Yap Kwan Seng at his own expense. Date: c 1910

[20]
Institute for Medical Research, Kuala Lumpur.

Cancellation: 1910
Back: Divided
Series and/or No.: 35
Publisher: The Federal Rubber Stamp Co., Kuala Lumpur

The Institute for Medical Research was founded in 1900 by Sir Frank Swettenham; it pioneered research in diseases such as malaria and beri-beri.

[21]
MALAY MOSQUE KUALA LUMPUR.

Cancellation: 1920
Back: Divided
Series and/or No.: 157
Publisher: M.S. Nakajima, Kuala Lumpur

The Masjid Jamek was built in 1909 at the confluence of the Klang and Gombak Rivers.

[22]
THE RAILWAY STATION IN KUALA LUMPUR.

Cancellation: Nil
Back: Divided
Publisher: G.R. Lambert & Co. Ltd, Singapore

The ppc shows a distant train approaching the old station. Date: c 1910

[23]
RAILWAY STATION, KUALA LUMPUR, F.M.S.

Cancellation: Nil
Back: Divided
Series and/or No.: 211
Publisher: M.S. Nakajima, Kuala Lumpur

A ppc in sepia tone showing the railway station, completed in 1910 (*right*), and the Malaya Railway Administration Building of 1917 (*left*).

[24]
RAIL WAY STATION OF KUALA LUMPUR, F.M.S.

Cancellation: 1913
Back: Divided
Publisher: M.S. Nakajima, Kuala Lumpur

It was designed by A.B. Hubback and completed in 1910 in the grand British "Raj" style.

[25]
Station Hotel F.M.S. Railway, Kuala Lumpur.

Cancellation: Nil
Back: Divided
Series and/or No.: 182
Publisher: M.S. Nakajima, Kuala Lumpur

The ppc shows the hotel's lounge, which is furnished with rattan furniture and plants on stands. Date: c 1920

[26]
Untitled [Interior of the Railway Station, KL].

Cancellation: Nil
Back: Divided

Date: c 1930

[27]
Kuala Lumpur, Station and F.M.S. Railway Offices.

Cancellation: 1927
Back: Divided
Series and/or No.: 522

The Railway Station is on the left while the FMS Railway Offices are on the right.

[28]
Railway Offices.

Cancellation: Nil
Back: Divided

A real photographic ppc showing the domes, minarets and arched windows of the railway offices. Date: c 1940

[29]
EMPIRE HOTEL, KUALA LUMPUR.
Cancellation: Nil
Back: Divided
Series and/or No.: 215
Publisher: The Federal Rubber Stamp Co., Kuala Lumpur

The Empire Hotel, which opened in 1909, became the Peninsular Hotel in 1919. Since 1973 it has been the office of the Malaysian Society of Architects. Date: c 1910

[30]
HOTEL MAJESTIC, KUALA LUMPUR.
Cancellation: Nil
Back: Divided
Publisher: Miyazaki Bros, Japan

The Majestic Hotel was opposite the Railway Station. Date: c 1930

[31]
TOWN OF KUALA LUMPUR, F.M.S.

Cancellation: 1913
Back: Divided
Series and/or No.: U.1
Publisher: M.S. Nakajima, Kuala Lumpur

This ppc shows a view of the Bangunan Sultan Abdul Samad and the Selangor Club, with the Padang in-between the two buildings.

[32]
SURVEY OFFICE, KUALA LUMPUR.

Cancellation: 1921
Back: Divided
Series and/or No.: 118
Publisher: M.S. Nakajima, Kuala Lumpur

The full magnificence of the Survey Office Building is shown in this ppc. The card is uncommon in that it was registered (15¢ rate) from Ipoh to USA.

[33]
Government Offices, Kuala Lumpur.

Cancellation: Nil
Back: Divided

The three greenish copper domes of the Bangunan Sultan Abdul Samad are highlighted in this ppc. Date: c 1920

[34]
Sanitary Board Offices, Kuala Lumpur.

Cancellation: Nil
Back: Divided

This building resembled the Bangunan Sultan Abdul Samad in terms of architectural style. Date: c 1920

[35]
TOWN HALL, KUALA LUMPUR.

Cancellation: Nil
Back: Divided
Series and/or No.: 194
Publisher: A. Kaulfuss, Penang

The building shown here in the early 1920s is the same as that described as the Sanitary Board Offices in the previous postcard.

[36]
F.M.S.R. GENERAL OFFICE, KUALA LUMPUR.

Cancellation: Nil
Back: Divided
Series and/or No.: 67

One of the ornate buildings housing the FMS Railway General Office. Date: c 1920

[37]
KUALA LUMPUR – THE SELANGOR CLUB.

Cancellation: 1906
Back: Divided
Publisher: G.R. Lambert & Co. Ltd, Singapore

The Selangor Club was founded in 1884; its building was completed in 1890. The President (ex-officio) was the Hon. British Resident.

[38]
PADANG & SELANGOR CLUB, KUALA LUMPUR, F.M.S.

Cancellation: 1926
Back: Divided
Series and/or No.: 133
Publisher: M.S. Nakajima, Kuala Lumpur

In the background is the Selangor Club, renovated in the early 20th century, while in the foreground is the beautiful Cops Fountain.

[39]
Kuala Lumpur—Chartered Bank.

Cancellation: Nil
Back: Divided
Series and/or No.: 21
Publisher: J. Brignon

This historic building was built in 1891 by A.C. Norman; it has housed the National Museum of History since 1996. Date: c 1910

[40]
Chartered Bank K.L.

Cancellation: Date unclear
Back: Divided

A photographic ppc of the Chartered Bank of India, Australia and China (predecessor of Standard Chartered Bank) situated at the junction of Jalan Raja and Jalan Sultan Hishamuddin. Date: c 1930

[41]
St Mary's Church, Kuala Lumpur, F.M.S.

Cancellation: 1915
Back: Divided

The Anglican Church (Church of St Mary the Virgin) at Jalan Raja was consecrated in 1895.

[42]
Church of St. Mary, the Virgin Kuala Lumpur.

Cancellation: Nil
Back: Divided
Series and/or No.: 125
Publisher: M.S. Nakajima, Kuala Lumpur

Date: c 1920

[43]
LAKE CLUB, KUALA LUMPUR.

Cancellation: Nil
Back: Divided
Series and/or No.: 15
Publisher: The Federal Rubber Stamp Co., Kuala Lumpur

An early view of the Lake Club soon after its founding in 1890.

[44]
KUALA LUMPUR – LAKE CLUB. SETTING ROOM.

Cancellation: 1920
Back: Divided
Series and/or No.: 36
Publisher: J. Brignon

The sitting room is furnished with cane furniture (popular with the Europeans during the colonial era). Notice the four *punkah* (fans) on the ceiling.

[45]
LAKE CLUB, KUALA LUMPUR, F.M.S.

Cancellation: Nil
Back: Divided
Publisher: M.S. Nakajima, Kuala Lumpur

This ppc shows the main clubhouse of the Lake Club. The pcc is unusual as it has serrated borders at its top and bottom. Date: c 1910

[46]
GOLF CLUB, KUALA LUMPUR.

Cancellation: 1910
Back: Divided
Series and/or No.: 286
Publisher: The Federal Rubber Stamp Co., Kuala Lumpur

The original Clubhouse at Petaling Hill – the area where the Victoria Institution, the Methodist Boys School, Stadium Merdeka and Stadium Negara now stand. Here, the Selangor Golf Club opened its course for play in 1893.

[47]
THE LAKE, KUALA LUMPUR, F.M.S.

Cancellation: 1907
Back: Divided
Series and/or No.: 3378

The Lake Gardens was the brainchild of Alfred Venning (Chairman of the Sanitary Board and State Treasurer of Selangor); in 1888 he proposed their development to Sir Frank Swettenham (then the Resident of Selangor).

[48]
GREETINGS FROM THE FAR EAST.

Cancellation: 1908
Back: Undivided
Publisher: G.R. Lambert & Co. Ltd, Singapore

This ppc depicts the lake in the Lake Gardens – a pier with a boat moored to it is in the foreground. A bridge is in the background.

[49]
Selangor Museum, Kuala Lumpur.

Cancellation: 1909
Back: Divided
Series and/or No.: 32
Publisher: The Federal Rubber Stamp Co., Kuala Lumpur

The Selangor Museum, the forerunner of the present Muzium Negara (National Museum). The origin of the National Museum dates back to 1887; the building in this ppc was built in 1906.

[50]
Museum, Kuala Lumpur.

Cancellation: Nil
Back: Divided
Series and/or No.: Art Collotype, No. 8
Publisher: Raphael Tuck & Sons, London

The Flemish-styled Selangor Museum is shown in this ppc; it was destroyed in 1945 by a stray bomb from an American plane.[15] Date: c 1910

[51]
CAPTAIN KUAN SENG'S GARDEN HOUSE, KUALA LUMPUR.

Cancellation: 1910
Back: Divided

Kapitan Yap Kwan Seng (1846–1901) was the last Kapitan Cina of Kuala Lumpur (1889–1901). He was a rich tin miner.

[52]
"CHANS" TEMPLE, KUALA LUMPUR.

Cancellation: Nil
Back: Divided

This is one of the many temples of the various dialect groups in prewar Selangor. Date: c 1910

[53]
"Ka Yin Hooi Kuan" (Hakka Kongsi), Sultan Street, Kuala Lumpur.

Cancellation: 1908
Back: Divided
Series and/or No.: 66
Publisher: The Federal Rubber Stamp Co., Kuala Lumpur

The temple was founded by Kapitan Yap Kwan Seng as a place of worship for the Hakka community in KL.

[54]
Catholic Church, Brickfields Road, Kuala Lumpur.

Cancellation: Nil
Back: Divided
Series and/or No.: 24
Publisher: The Federal Rubber Stamp Co., Kuala Lumpur

This is the Church of the Holy Rosary; at the time of this ppc, the central spire had not yet been built. Date: 1904

[55]
Race Course, Ampang Road, Kuala Lumpur.

Cancellation: 1909
Back: Divided
Series and/or No.: 62
Publisher: The Federal Rubber Stamp Co., Kuala Lumpur

A scarce bi-view ppc of the Race Course; the top view shows the race track, the bottom view shows the grandstand.

[56]
Race Course, Kuala Lumpur.

Cancellation: Nil
Back: Divided
Series and/or No.: 220
Publisher: The Federal Rubber Stamp Co., Kuala Lumpur

Horse-racing began in Selangor in the early 1890s under the patronage of Sir William Maxwell, who was then the British Resident.[15]
Date: c 1910

[57]
THE RACE-COURSE OF KUALA LUMPUR.

Cancellation: Nil
Back: Divided
Publisher: G.R. Lambert & Co. Ltd, Singapore

Horse-racing was very popular, as evidenced by the crowds at the Race Course. The race track has now been replaced by the Petronas Twin Towers. Date: c 1910

[58]
AMPANG ROAD, KUALA LUMPUR, F.M.S.

Cancellation: 1921
Back: Divided
Series and/or No.: 169
Publisher: M.S. Nakajima, Kuala Lumpur

Ampang (Dam) Road was so named as it was an early mining site.

[59]
BRICKFIELDS ROAD, KUALA LUMPUR.

Cancellation: Nil
Back: Divided

The road derived its name from the many brick kilns that were located there in the 1880s. Today the road has been renamed Jalan Tun Sambanthan.[15] Date: c 1920

[60]
EMBANKMENT, KUALA LUMPUR.

Cancellation: 1932
Back: Divided

The dome of the clock tower of the Bangunan Sultan Abdul Samad is seen in the background.

Church Street, Kuala Lumpur.

[61]
CHURCH STREET, KUALA LUMPUR.

Cancellation: Nil
Back: Divided
Series and/or No.: 77
Publisher: The Federal Rubber Stamp Co., Kuala Lumpur

Notice the absence of traffic – a lone rickshaw is pictured alongside a row of terrace houses. Date: 1909

Holland Road, Kuala Lumpur.

[62]
HOLLAND ROAD, KUALA LUMPUR.

Cancellation: Nil
Back: Divided
Series and/or No.: 67
Publisher: The Federal Rubber Stamp Co., Kuala Lumpur

This ppc shows a three-storey commercial building by the river. Date: c 1910

[63]
JAVA STREET, KUALA LUMPUR.

Cancellation: Nil
Back: Divided

Java Street was named after the Malays who settled there; it was later renamed Mountbatten Road (and now Jalan Tun Perak). The building is that of Whiteaway, Laidlaw & Co. Date: c 1910

[64]
OLD MARKET SQUARE, KUALA LUMPUR.

Cancellation: 1926
Back: Divided

Now called Medan Pasar, this was the gambling centre in Kuala Lumpur during the 1900s. Yap Ah Loy (the third Kapitan Cina of Kuala Lumpur) owned many casinos and brothels there. The large building at the far end is the Hongkong and Shanghai Bank. It was replaced by a new building in the 1960s.

[65]

Petaling Street, K. Lumpur.

Cancellation: Nil
Back: Divided

Originally Kuala Lumpur's main shopping area, Petaling Street was one of the first roads to be named. Petaling is the name of a hardwood tree, though the Chinese refer to the street as *Shu Chong Kai* (Cantonese for "tapioca factory road").[15] Date: c 1930

[66]

Pudu St., K.L.

Cancellation: Nil
Back: Divided
Publisher: Sun Studio

Pudu is the name of a small tree. The street was lined with many Chinese shops. Date: c 1935

[67]
CONVENT, KUALA LUMPUR, SELANGOR.

Cancellation: Nil
Back: Divided
Series and/or No.: 153
Publisher: The Federal Rubber Stamp Co., Kuala Lumpur

This ppc shows the convent school building (*right*) and a grotto (with a statue of the Virgin Mary) on the left. Date: c 1900

[68]
ST. JOHN SCHOOL K. LUMPUR.

Cancellation: Nil
Back: Divided

The school was founded by the Roman Catholic missionaries in 1906; the impressive school building in Bukit Nanas shown in this ppc was completed in 1907. Date: c 1930

[69]
METHODIST BOY'S SCHOOL, KUALA LUMPUR.
Cancellation: 1909
Back: Divided
Series and/or No.: 151
Publisher: The Federal Rubber Stamp Co., Kuala Lumpur

This impressive school building is that of the Methodist Boys' School at Petaling Hill.

[70]
METHODIST GIRLS' SCHOOL, KUALA LUMPUR.
Cancellation: 1914
Back: Divided
Series and/or No.: 188
Publisher: The Federal Rubber Stamp Co., Kuala Lumpur

This was a Day and Boarding School for girls at High Street (near the Railway Station).

[71]
VICTORIA INSTITUTION K. LUMPUR.

Cancellation: Nil
Back: Divided
Publisher: Yano & Co.

Victoria Institution was opened in 1894. The ppc shows the main building and clock tower (designed by A.C. Norman) on Shaw Road (now known as Jalan Hang Tuah) built in 1929.[15]
Date: c 1930

[72]
THE SLAUGHTER HOUSE, KUALA LUMPUR.

Cancellation: Nil
Back: Divided
Series and/or No.: 63
Publisher: The Federal Rubber Stamp Co., Kuala Lumpur

A ppc with two views of the Abattoir; the poor cow outside is waiting to be slaughtered!
Date: c 1905

[73]
FEDERAL HOUSE FOR WOMEN AND GIRLS, KUALA LUMPUR.
METHODIST BOYS' SCHOOL, KUALA LUMPUR.

Cancellation: Nil
Back: Divided
Series and/or No.: 148
Publisher: The Federal Rubber Stamp Co., Kuala Lumpur

A black-and-white ppc with two views, the Federal House and Boys' School were run by the Methodist Mission. Date: c 1910

[74]
BATU CAVES, KUALA LUMPUR.

Cancellation: 1931
Back: Divided
Publisher: The Federal Rubber Stamp Co., Kuala Lumpur

The caves consist of three main limestone caves; they were discovered by William Hornaday in 1878. The Batu Caves are in Selayang, 13 km north of Kuala Lumpur.

[75]

KUALA KUBU, SELANGOR.

Cancellation: Nil
Back: Divided
Series and/or No.: 191
Publisher: A. Kaulfuss, Penang

Kuala Kubu (the Stockade at the junction of two rivers) is the district capital of Hulu Selangor and is located on top of a hill. In 1883 the town was destroyed by a great flood caused by a broken dam near the town. After the tragedy a new town (shown in ppc) was built nearby. Date: c 1910

[76]

REST HOUSE THE GAP, SELANGOR.

Cancellation: Nil
Back: Divided
Series and/or No.: M.68
Publisher: M.S. Nakajima, Kuala Lumpur

This is the area at the bottom of Fraser's Hill. It offered a cool respite for the Europeans in prewar Malaya. Date: c 1930

[77]
Hot Spring, Setapak, Selangor.
Cancellation: 1914
Back: Divided
Series and/or No.: 254
Publisher: The Federal Rubber Stamp Co., Kuala Lumpur

This sepia ppc shows two bathers at the hot spring.

[78]
Hot Spring, Dusun Tua Sanatorium, Ulu Langat.
Cancellation: 1912
Back: Divided
Publisher: The Federal Rubber Stamp Co., Kuala Lumpur

Dusun Tua is in the district of Hulu Langat, Selangor. In the 1900s it had a hot spring and sanatorium for those convalescing from diseases such as tuberculosis.

[79]
Rest House, Kajang, Selangor.

Cancellation: 1913
Back: Divided
Series and/or No.: M.45
Publisher: M.S. Nakajima, Kuala Lumpur

Kajang (Malay for "a palm leaf boat canopy") is about 20 km south of Kuala Lumpur; it was founded in 1807 after the Klang war. Famous for its satay, it is also called "Satay Town".

[80]
Sea Shore, Morib, Selangor.

Cancellation: Nil
Back: Divided
Series and/or No.: 8
Publisher: M.S. Nakajima, Kuala Lumpur

For those seeking a serene retreat from the bustle of Kuala Lumpur, Morib is just the place. This view dates from c 1920. Situated at the southern end of Selangor, it is about one and a half hours drive from Kuala Lumpur. The Allied forces landed on this beach in 1945.

[81]
SULTAN'S ISTANA AND RACE COURSE, KLANG.

Cancellation: Nil
Back: Divided
Series and/or No.: 89
Publisher: The Federal Rubber Stamp Co., Kuala Lumpur

The racecourse is in the foreground; the Sultan's palace is in the background. The racetrack was completed in 1903 by the Klang Gymkhana Club.[16]
Date: c 1905

[82]
RAILWAY STATION, KLANG.

Cancellation: Nil
Back: Divided
Series and/or No.: 98
Publisher: The Federal Rubber Stamp Co., Kuala Lumpur

Klang was connected to Kuala Lumpur by rail in 1886. This card dates from c 1900.

[83]
DISTRICT OFFICE, KLANG.

Cancellation: Nil
Back: Divided
Series and/or No.: 91
Publisher: The Federal Rubber Stamp Co., Kuala Lumpur

The building is a two-storey building built on elevated brick columns. Date: c 1900

[84]
P.W.D. KLANG.

Cancellation: Nil
Back: Divided
Series and/or No.: 100
Publisher: The Federal Rubber Stamp Co., Kuala Lumpur

This is a handsome single-storey building which housed the Public Works Department (PWD); two gardeners are clearing the lawn. Date: c 1910

[85]
KLANG CLUB, KLANG, SELANGOR.

Cancellation: Nil
Back: Divided
Series and/or No.: M.43
Publisher: M.S. Nakajima, Kuala Lumpur

The Klang Club was situated beside the Race Course. Before the grandstand of the Race Course was completed in 1903, the Klang Club served instead.[16] Date: c 1910

[86]
ON THE KLANG RIVER, KLANG.

Cancellation: Nil
Back: Divided
Series and/or No.: 95
Publisher: The Federal Rubber Stamp Co., Kuala Lumpur

The Klang River divides the town into two halves; in the late 1880s and early 1900s the river connected Klang to Kuala Lumpur. In this ppc, passengers are embarking on a small boat. Date: c 1910

[87]
Railway Station, Port Swettenham.

Cancellation: 1913
Back: Divided
Series and/or No.: 186
Publisher: The Federal Rubber Stamp Co., Kuala Lumpur

On 15 September 1886, the whole of Kuala Lumpur gathered to celebrate the opening of the railway line from Kuala Lumpur to Klang.[15] The line was later extended to Port Swettenham.

[88]
Shipping Offices and Overhead Railway Bridge, Port Swettenham.

Cancellation: Nil
Back: Divided
Series and/or No.: 82
Publisher: The Federal Rubber Stamp Co., Kuala Lumpur

The message on the back reads: "This is a small port we called at on our way to and from Penang." Date: c 1910

[89]
POLICE STATION AND MARINE OFFICE, PORT SWETTENHAM.

Cancellation: Nil
Back: Divided
Series and/or No.: 79
Publisher: The Federal Rubber Stamp Co., Kuala Lumpur

The buildings in the ppc are single-storeyed and were built on elevated concrete columns.
Date: c 1910

[90]
THE JETTY, PORT SWETTENHAM.

Cancellation: 1910
Back: Divided
Series and/or No.: 85
Publisher: The Federal Rubber Stamp Co., Kuala Lumpur

A large steamship with a tall funnel is anchored at the pier.

[91]
Port Swettenham. The S.S. Malacca.

Cancellation: Nil
Back: Divided
Series and/or No.: 4
Publisher: J. Brignon

The SS *Malacca* was one of the steamers that plied the coast of Malaya during the prewar years. Date: c 1920

[92]
Port Swettenham, Selangor, F.M.S.

Cancellation: Nil
Back: Divided
Series and/or No.: 162
Publisher: M.S. Nakajima, Kuala Lumpur

A sepia-toned ppc showing the port crowded with a steamship, numerous *sampans* and small boats. Date: c 1930

[93]
MALAYA – RUBBER-COOLIES BRINGING IN LATEX.

Cancellation: Nil
Back: Divided
Publisher: McCorquodale & Co. Ltd, London

Many migrants came from India to work in the labour-intensive rubber estates and factories. Date: c 1910

[94]
KEUT ESTATE, 3½ YEARS RUBBUR.

Cancellation: 1913
Back: Divided
Series and/or No.: M.34
Publisher: M.S. Nakajima, Kuala Lumpur

In the 1900s the rubber industry grew rapidly in Selangor. Large estates such as the Keut Estate were owned by Europeans and the Chinese.

[95]
TIN MINING, SUNGEI BESI.

Cancellation: Nil
Back: Divided
Series and/or No.: 76

Tin-mining brought great wealth to Selangor and Malaya. The Sungei Besi mine (15 km south of Kuala Lumpur) was a large tin mine in Selangor. Though initially owned by the Kapitan Cina, the mine was later acquired by Messers Foo Choo Choon and Mons. Edgar.[16] Date: c 1910

[96]
TIN MINING IN ULU SELANGOR, SELANGOR.

Cancellation: Nil
Back: Divided
Series and/or No.: 146
Publisher: The Federal Rubber Stamp Co., Kuala Lumpur

An open cast mine in Ulu Selangor. Mining was initially done on a small scale by the Malays. Later, many migrants from China came to work on the tin mines. Date: c 1910

[97]
OPEN CAST TIN MINE, SELANGOR.
Cancellation: 1928
Back: Divided
Publisher: Houghton Butcher (Eastern) Ltd, Singapore

A European man and Chinese workers are shown in the central hut in the open cast tin mine.

[98]
SHOOTING TIGER, SELANGOR, F.M.S.
Cancellation: Nil
Back: Divided
Series and/or No.: M.81
Publisher: M.S. Nakajima, Kuala Lumpur

During the 1900s, tigers roamed freely in the jungles of Selangor and the rest of Malaya. Today the only tigers that can be seen in Selangor are those in the zoo and on postage stamps.

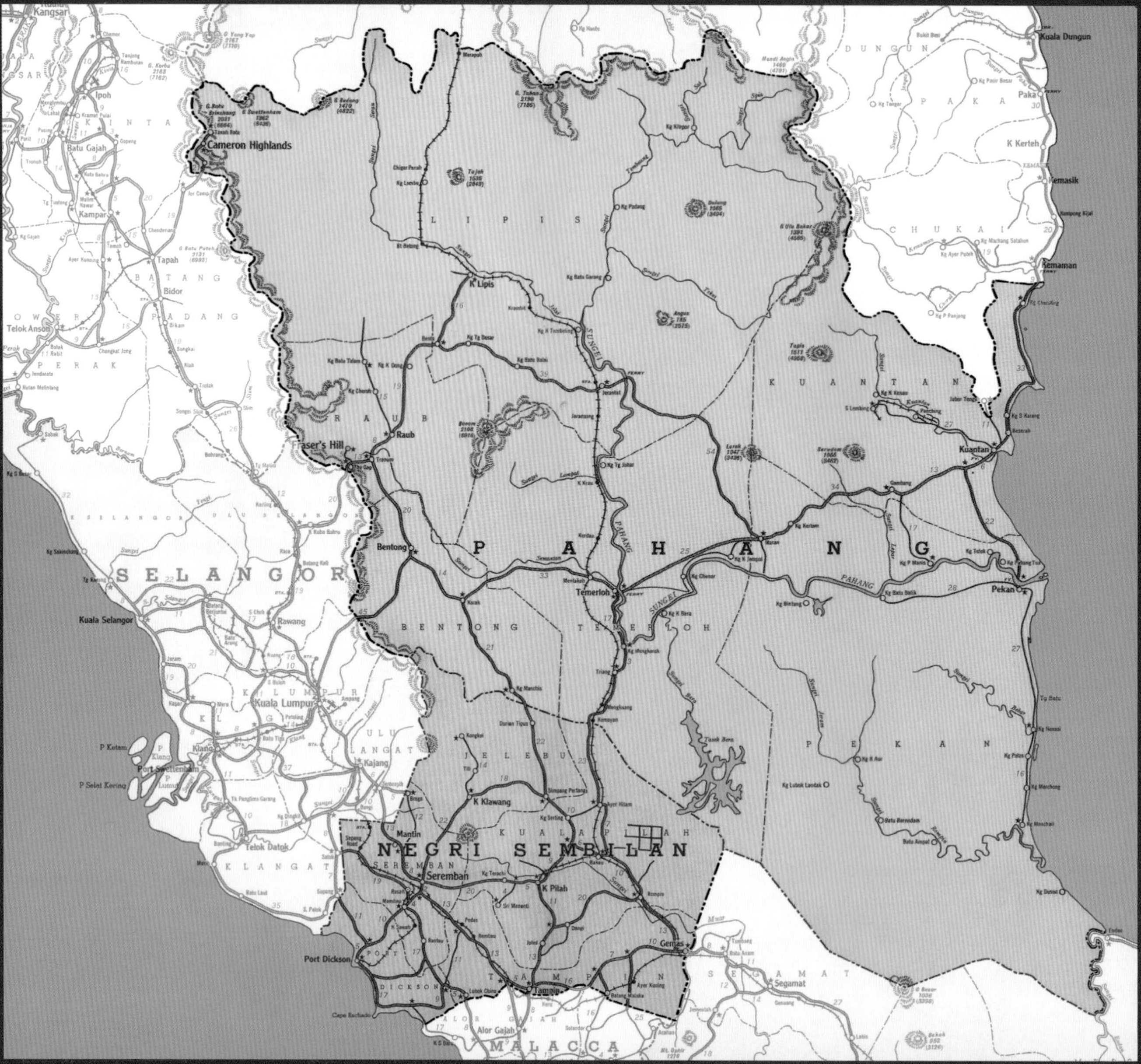
PAHANG
SELANGOR
NEGRI SEMBILAN
MALACCA
LIPIS
RAUB
BENTONG
TEMERLOH
KUANTAN
PEKAN
JELEBU
KUALA PILAH
SEREMBAN
PORT DICKSON
TAMPIN
KLANG
ULU LANGAT
KUALA LUMPUR
ULU SELANGOR
BATANG PADANG
KINTA
PERAK
DUNGUN
PAKA
CHUKAI
SEGAMAT
Kuala Kangsar
Ipoh
Batu Gajah
Kampar
Tapah
Bidor
Telok Anson
Cameron Highlands
K Lipis
Raub
Fraser's Hill
Bentong
Temerloh
Maran
Kuantan
Pekan
Kuala Dungun
Paka
K Kerteh
Kemasik
Kemaman
Kuala Selangor
Rawang
Kuala Lumpur
Klang
Port Swettenham
Kajang
Telok Datok
Mantin
Seremban
K Klawang
K Pilah
Gemas
Port Dickson
Tampin
Alor Gajah
Segamat
P Ketam
P Selat Kering

NEGRI SEMBILAN and PAHANG

Negri Sembilan

The state of Negri Sembilan (NS), translated literally as "nine states", is so called because it consists of nine separate districts (or *nagari*). The Arabic honorific of the state is Darul Khusus ("Special Abode").[20] NS is bounded on its north by Selangor and Pahang, with Johore to its east, and Malacca to its south.

NS, also known as the "Land of Quiet Grace", is often associated with the pervasive influence of the Minangkabau, a tribe of migrants from Sumatra. This can be seen in the unique horn-shaped roofs on many of its buildings. The Minangkabau brought with them their *adat* or traditions, which include matrilineal kinship.[20]

The history of NS has been well-documentated.[12, 21] British intervention in 1874 led to the unification of its various tribal factions under the Yamtuan (now known as the Yang di-Pertuan Negeri Sembilan) as the paramount ruler of the confederacy in 1898. Tuanku Muhammad Shah [99] became the Yamtuan in 1898; he was succeeded by his son, Tuanku Abdul Rahman in 1933 [100]. Tuanku Abdul Rahman became the first Yang di-Pertuan Agong of Malaya in 1957. The sons of the Yamtuan are shown in [101].

With the formation of the FMS, a British Resident was appointed to the state of Negri Sembilan, who wielded most of the political power. Martin Lister was the first British Resident and he held this position from 1895 to 1897.[12] His house in Seremban [102 (*upper right*)] rivals in splendour the Istana (Sri Menanti) of the Yamtuan.

The name "Seremban" may be a corrupted form of the Malay word *beremban* (a mist which lay over old tin mines). Prewar visitors often travelled to Seremban by train; it was linked by rail to Prai (Province Wellesley) by 1903. Like many other railway stations in major towns, Seremban's railway station also had a hotel [103] within its premises. The post and telegraph office [104] was near the railway station, as were the Central Police Station and the Court House [105-106]. Cards show various scenes and buildings in prewar Seremban [107-114]; a war memorial to honour the dead soldiers of the First World War (1914–1918) was erected in front of the State's Secretariat [117].

Jungle products were important to the economy of NS; one of these was *damar* (resin) from the giant forest trees [118].

Port Dickson [115; 116 (*lower right*)] was named after Sir Frederick Dickson in 1890, when Sir Frederick was the acting Governor of the Straits Settlements. As its name implies, it is a seaport. Port Dickson lies 32 kilometres southwest of Seremban. It is also a popular seaside resort.

The Pengkalan Kempas Historical Complex [123] is situated 35 kilometres from Port Dickson, and is famous for its three mysterious megalithic stones which, due to their shapes, are known as "The Rudder", "The Sword" and "The Spoon". Believed to have been created in the 2nd–3rd century, some have Arab and Sumatran scripts carved into them. Local myth has it that these stones are imbued with special powers which allow them to grow during the night.[22]

The Orang Asli, aboriginal people of the Malay Peninsula, were mostly found in south Perak, Selangor, Pahang and NS [130].[16] Today, their descendants are so widely scattered among the villages that their bloodline can no longer be considered pure.

The residence of the British Resident in Seremban was very grand.
(*See* [102])

Many coolies are waiting at the wooden wharf; a warehouse is in the background.
(*See* [116])

The Orang Asli are indigenous people of Malaya; they are skilled hunters who use blowpipes for hunting.
(*See* [129])

The Raub Australian Gold Mines Ltd operated one of the many gold mines in Pahang during the late 1880s.
(*See* [133])

Pahang

Pahang was, in terms of land area, the largest component of the FMS and is the largest state in the Malay Peninsula. It is bordered to its north by Kelantan, to its west by Perak, Selangor and Negri Sembilan, to its south by Johore and to its east by Trengganu and the South China Sea. The Arabic honorific of Pahang is Darul Makmur ("Abode of Tranquillity"); the state capital is Kuantan.

Dutch influence in Pahang had declined by 1795 and ended in 1824 with the signing of the Anglo-Dutch Treaty. Domestic turmoil eventually led to the appointment of a British Resident (J.P. Rodger) in 1888. Sultan Ahmad ruled Pahang as Bendahara from 1863 to 1884 and as Sultan from 1884 to 1914.[12] Sultans Abdullah and Sir Abu Bakar, who ruled from 1919 to 1932, and 1932 to 1974 respectively, are shown in [119] and [120].

Much of prewar Pahang was covered in thick vegetation, with a ridge of granite hills running along its western boundaries. Through the intervening valley ran the tributaries of the Tembeling and Jelai Rivers, which commingled in the plains below to form the broad Pahang River.[12] Many Malays lived in house boats on the Pahang River [121; 122]. Fishing and bathing were also common activities along the Jelai River [124; 125]. In contrast, many of the Orang Asli lived in the hills and jungles [126; 127]. The Orang Asli are skilled hunters who use blowpipes for hunting [128]; they were described as having distinctive features and they were known occasionally to cultivate plots of land [129 (*upper left*)].

The terrain in Pahang is hilly and was covered in thick jungle; roads [131; 132] were cut on hilly slopes through the jungle.

Gold was mined in Pahang from the late 1880s [134; 135] but by the 1920s, only the Raub Australian Gold Mines Ltd remained [133 (*lower left*)]. In the 1920s, it produced about 14,000 oz of gold a year, a small amount compared to previous yields. Prewar Pahang had many rubber estates as well [137].

Sungai Lembing [138] was a tin-mining town 42 kilometres northwest of Kuantan in Pahang. *Sungai* is the Malay word for "river" while *lembing* means "spear". Legend has it that a local ruler had a vision of a spear in the nearby river, hence its name. Until the 1970s, Sungai Lembing was a major producer of underground tin. Indeed, it was once regarded as the richest town in Pahang, and it was known as the El Dorado of the East. Today, the town has been turned into a tourist destination, with old tin mines being converted into museums.

During the colonial era, Pahang was well-known for its cool hill stations of Fraser's Hill and Cameron Highlands (a "hill station" was a town at a relatively high elevation, generally cooler and therefore offering relief from the tropical heat); Genting Highlands was developed after the Second World War and is today the location of a mountain resort. Fraser's Hill [139–143] was named after Louis James Fraser, a Scotsman who prospected for gold in Australia but ended up mining tin ore here during the 1890s. He mysteriously disappeared one day; there were rumours that his disappearance was linked to the opium and gambling den he founded and managed. Tin ore eventually ran out in 1913, but Fraser's Hill enjoyed a second lease of life, thanks to its 1524-metre elevation and its lush valley below. In 1917, it was redeveloped as a colonial hill resort and by 1922, a road had been cut through the mountains to the valley. This led to the construction of many European-style bungalows.

Cameron Highlands [144] was founded in 1885 by William Cameron, a government surveyor who had, on one of his surveys, discovered a plateau with an elevation of 1370–1700 metres above sea level. However, some 20 years were to go by before the first pioneers settled down in the area. Thanks to its cool climate, Cameron Highlands offers the ideal conditions in which to grow tea, flowers and vegetables.[24]

[99]
Untitled [Tuanku Muhammad Shah].

Cancellation: Nil
Back: Divided

Tuanku Muhammad Shah was the Yamtuan of Negri Sembilan from 1898 to 1933. He is pictured with a royal umbrella bearer at Istana Sri Menanti, the royal palace. Date: c 1920

[100]
Untitled [Tuanku Abdul Rahman].

Cancellation: Nil
Back: Divided

The Tuanku succeeded his father, Tuanku Muhammad Shah, in 1933. Shown here in 1950, he became the First Yang di-Pertuan Agong of Malaya in 1957.

[101]
Untitled [The sons of the Yamtuan].

Cancellation: 1913
Back: Divided
Publisher: S. Kurita, Japan

Possibly Tuanku Muhammad's two eldest sons, Abdul Aziz (1894–1917) and Abdul Rahman (1895–1960).

[102]
Resident's House Seremban.

Cancellation: 1913
Back: Divided

The British Resident in Seremban from 1895 to 1941 wielded more power than the Yamtuan. As was to be expected, the British Resident's mansion was very grand.

[103]
Untitled [The Railway Station and hotel].

Cancellation: 1913
Back: Divided
Publisher: S. Kurita, Japan

The Railway Station at Seremban was built in 1903. The message on the back of the ppc reads: "The card I am sending you is the Railway Station where I am staying."

[104]
SEREMBAN. POST & TELEGRAPH OFFICE.

Cancellation: 1908
Back: Divided

The office was originally designated Sungai Ujong (1879–1894) before the formation of Negri Sembilan as a postal authority. The Seremban post office started in 1899.

[105]
CENTRAL POLICE STATION, SEREMBAN.

Cancellation: Nil
Back: Divided
Series and/or No.: 107
Publisher: The Federal Rubber Stamp Co., Kuala Lumpur

Notice the absence of traffic on the street. The Chinese (*foreground*) and Malay men (*in front of police station*) are wearing hats. Date: c 1910

[106]
THE COURT HOUSE, SEREMBAN.

Cancellation: Nil
Back: Divided
Publisher: G.R. Lambert & Co. Ltd, Singapore

The Court House is a handsome colonial-styled single-storey building. Date: c 1910

[107]
Untitled [Main street and shopping centre].

Cancellation: Nil
Back: Divided

The street was named Birch Road in 1906 in honour of Edward Birch, the second Resident of Negri Sembilan.

[108]
Untitled [Anglo-Chinese School].

Cancellation: Nil
Back: Divided
Publisher: K. Murai, Seremban

The message on this ppc reads: "This is the Anglo-Chinese School where my elder sister is teaching. We go there in the evenings to play ping-pong, croquet or tennis... This is a boys' school and a large number of Chinese boys go to it." Date: 1923

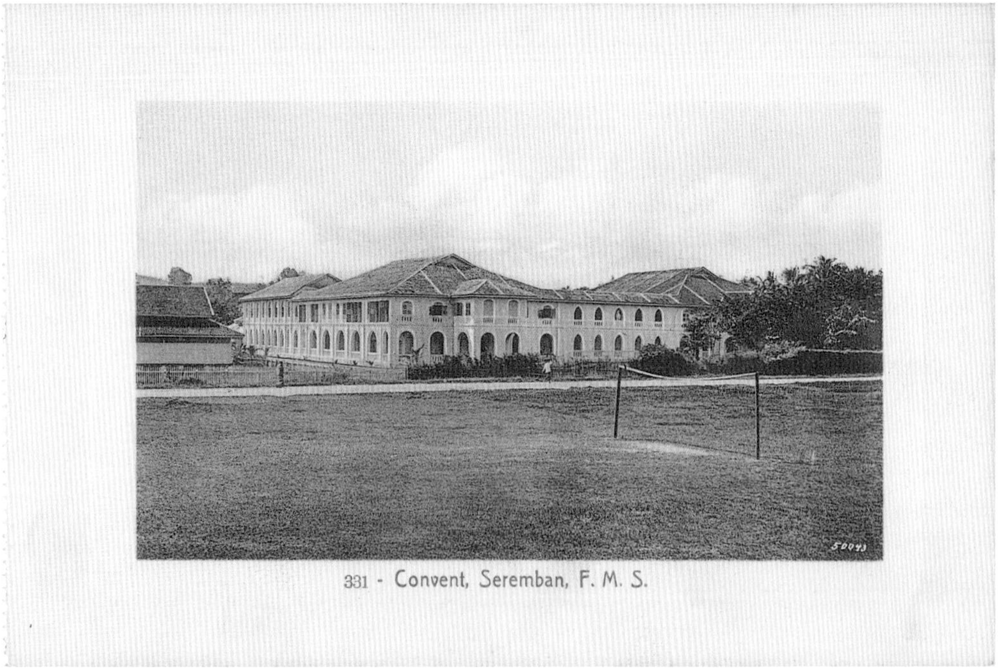

[109]
Convent, Seremban, F.M.S.

Cancellation: Nil
Back: Divided
Series and/or No.: 331
Publisher: The Federal Rubber Stamp Co., Kuala Lumpur

The school is shown with its playing field in the foreground. Date: c 1910

[110]
Untitled [Convent School].

Cancellation: Nil
Back: Divided
Publisher: K Murai, Seremban

The message on the back of the ppc reads: "This is the Convent School where my sisters go to... There are a few boarders and a large number of orphans." Date: 1923

[111]
SEREMBAN – EN TOURNÉE APOSTOLIQUE.

Cancellation: Nil
Back: Divided
Series and/or No.: Phototypie Lescuyer, 16
Publisher: Remparts-d'Ainay, Lyon

Nuns from the Convent School being pulled in a rickshaw. Note the varicose veins on the legs of the rickshaw puller. Date: c 1910

[112]
Untitled [The Sungai Ujong Club].

Cancellation: Nil
Back: Divided

The message behind reads: "The entrance to the Sungai Ujong Club. The road leading on to the right is Bathurst Road, where we formerly lived." In the 1900s there were two European clubs in Seremban: the Negri Sembilan Cub and the Sungai Ujong Club. Date: c 1910

[113]
Public Gardens, Seremban, N. Sembilan.

Cancellation: Nil
Back: Divided
Series and/or No.: 137
Publisher: The Federal Rubber Stamp Co.,
Kuala Lumpur

The Public Gardens (or Lake Gardens) have two lakes; they were (and still are) popular with residents and visitors. Date: 1909

[114]
Untitled [A typical house in Seremban].

Cancellation: Nil
Back: Divided

The Minangkabau tradition in Negri Sembilan is typified by the horn-shaped roofs of its buildings. Date: c 1930

[115]
Untitled [Main street in Port Dickson].

Cancellation: Nil
Back: Divided

The street is deserted except for two motorcars; the shop sign on the left reads "Guthrie & Co. Ltd/incorporated in the Colony of Singapore". Date: c 1940

[116]
Coolies at Wharf, Port Dickson.

Cancellation: 1920
Back: Divided
Publisher: The Federal Rubber Stamp Co., Kuala Lumpur

Many coolies are waiting at the wooden wharf; a warehouse is in the background.

[117]
Untitled [The War Memorial].

Cancellation: Nil
Back: Divided

The War Memorial at Seremban was constructed in memory of the dead of the First World War. It was built in front of the State's Secretariat (which is now the State Library). Date: 1931

[118]
MALAYAN DAMAR PENAL CLIMBING WITH POLE.

Cancellation: Nil
Back: Divided

The giant forest trees found in many parts of the FMS including Negri Sembilan produce a valuable resin. Using a pole, the Malays climb up the tree to tap its resin sap. Date: c 1930

[119]
Untitled [Sultan Abdullah of Pahang].

Cancellation: Nil
Back: Divided

Sultan Abdullah succeeded to the throne in 1917 and was installed in 1919.

[120]
Untitled [Sultan Sir Abu Bakar of Pahang].

Cancellation: Nil
Back: Divided

A real black-and-white photographic ppc (c 1940) showing Sultan Sir Abu Bakar saluting at Pekan, the royal capital of Pahang. He reigned from 1932 to 1974.

[121]

SINGAPORE. SCENE FROM THE PAHANG RIVER.

Cancellation: 1908
Back: Divided
Publisher: Max H. Hilcks, Singapore

The caption is incorrect; the Pahang River is in Pahang and not in Singapore!

[122]

HOUSE BOATS, PAHANG.

Cancellation: Nil
Back: Divided
Series and/or No.: 9315
Publisher: Houghton Butcher (Eastern) Ltd, Singapore

Many Malays lived in house boats anchored along the bank of the Pahang River. This ppc was sold at the Malaya Pavilion of the 1924 British Empire Exhibition.

[123]
ANCIENT MONOLITHS AT PENGKALEN KEMPAS, NEGRI SEMBILAN.

Cancellation: 1923
Back: Divided

These three mysterious megalithic stones were carved in the 2nd–3rd century. They are at Pengkalan Kempas, 35 km from Port Dickson.

[124]
SUNGEI JELAI, PAHANG.

Cancellation: Nil
Back: Divided
Series and/or No.: 9122
Publisher: Houghton Butcher (Eastern) Ltd, Singapore.

This ppc shows people bathing in the Jelai River. The ppc was sold at the Malaya Pavilion of the 1924 British Empire Exhibition.

[125]
ON THE SUNGAI JELAI, PAHANG.

Cancellation: 1930
Back: Divided
Series and/or No.: 9310

This black-and-white real photographic ppc shows three Malays on a boat on the Jelai River.

[126]
PAHANG. SAKAI DWELLING.

Cancellation: Nil
Back: Divided
Publisher: Wilson & Co., Singapore.

This ppc shows a view of the treetop dwelling of the Orang Asli in Pahang. Date: c 1910

[127]
PAHANG GROUP OF SAKAIS.

Cancellation: 1908
Back: Divided
Publisher: Wilson & Co., Singapore.

An European man with hat (likely to be a gold or tin miner) posing with a group of Orang Asli; his name could have possibly been "Tom" (written on his shirt).

[128]
NATIVE SACKAI PEOPLE, F.M.S.

Cancellation: 1912
Back: Divided
Series and/or No.: 71

The Orang Asli were (and still are) skilled hunters who used blowpipes for hunting.

[129]
NATIVE SACKAI PEOPLE, F.M.S.

Cancellation: Nil
Back: Divided

The Orang Asli often cultivated the lands (the man in the middle appears to be holding a *cangkul*). They also hunted and fished.
Date: c 1915

[130]
SAKAI, ULU JELEBU, NEGRI SEMBILAN.

Cancellation: 1928
Back: Divided

The Orang Asli are the aboriginal people of Malaya; this real photographic ppc shows a group of Orang Asli in the jungle of Ulu Jelebu, northern Negri Sembilan.

[131]
TRUNK ROAD, PAHANG, F.M.S.
Cancellation: Nil
Back: Divided
This sepia ppc shows a winding road going up a hill. A lorry carrying logs (*top*) and a motorcar (*bottom*) are pictured in the card. Date: c 1920

[132]
TRUNK ROAD PAHANG.
Cancellation: Nil
Back: Divided
Series and/or No.: 21
Publisher: M.S. Nakajima, Kuala Lumpur
In the midst of the jungle, two cars can be seen crawling up the hilly road. Date: c 1920

[133]
RAUB AUSTRALIAN GOLD MINES, LTD., PAHANG.

Cancellation: 1924
Back: Divided
Series and/or No.: 312
Publisher: Houghton Butcher (Eastern) Ltd, Singapore

Gold was mined in Pahang from the late 1880s, but by the 1930s only the Raub Australian Gold Mines Ltd still functioned.

[134]
SINGAPORE. GOLD MINE IN PAHANG.

Cancellation: 1907
Back: Divided
Series and/or No.: 162

The notation is erroneous, Pahang is in Malaya, not Singapore. The gold mine shown on the slope of the hill is likely to be that of the Raub Australian Gold Mines Ltd.

[135]
MINING CAMP, PAHANG.
Cancellation: Nil
Back: Divided
Series and/or No.: 3140
Publisher: Houghton Butcher (Eastern) Ltd, Singapore

A gold mining camp situated on a hill. The buildings are made of wood and have attap roofs. Date: 1934

[136]
CLIFF TIN MINE, PAHANG.
Cancellation: Nil
Back: Divided
Series and/or No.: 913
Publisher: Houghton Butcher (Eastern) Ltd, Singapore

Hills were uncommon locations for tin-mining, as most tin-mining activities in Malaya took place in valleys and on the plains. Date: c 1920

[137]
Views & Rubber Estates of Kuantan Pahang F.M.S.

Cancellation: Nil
Back: Divided

This photographic ppc has 13 views of rubber estates in Pahang: some of the estates' names were Kuala Reman Estate, Semambu Estate, Sungai Talam Estate, Atlur Estate and Ruby Estate. Date: c 1930

[138]
Untitled [Sungai Lembing].

Cancellation: 1930
Back: Divided

The message on the back of this ppc reads: "This is a funny bridge we walked over when we went to Sungai Lembing. It is very wobbly in the middle."

[139]
Ah Joon Shop Keeper General Store Fraser Hill.

Cancellation: 1930
Back: Divided
Series and/or No.: 4

The message on the back of the ppc reads: "Having a topping time recuperating after a year's hard toil. Four rounds of golf every day..."

[140]
Main Road Post Office Dispensary and Ah Joon Shop Fraser's Hill.

Cancellation: Nil
Back: Divided
Series and/or No.: 24

This photographic ppc shows the post office (*left*) in Fraser's Hill; the Dispensary and Ah Joon Shop are shown in the previous card. In the foreground is a lawn with children playing. The roads are crowded with motorcars. Date: 1931

[141]
VICTORY HOUSE FRASER'S HILL.

Cancellation: 1932
Back: Divided
Series and/or No.: 4

"Victory House" is the name of this handsome colonial bungalow in Fraser's Hill.

[142]
"RETREAT" THE FRASER'S HILL.

Cancellation: 1934
Back: Divided
Series and/or No.: 18

The message on the back of this ppc reads: "This little house... it belongs to the Church of England. Played quite a bit of golf and bridge. It is glorious being in the cool air..."

[143]
Untitled [Selangor Club, Fraser's Hill].

Cancellation: 1934
Back: Divided

On the back of the ppc is written: "This is the Selangor Club, Fraser's Hill and you can see the tennis courts and Padang... Did a lot of walking."

[144]
Untitled [Cameron Highlands Hotel and Golf Course].

Cancellation: 1939
Back: Divided

On the ppc's back is scribbled: "We are staying in the little bungalow above the hotel, and thoroughly enjoying the change... The weather is very kind..."

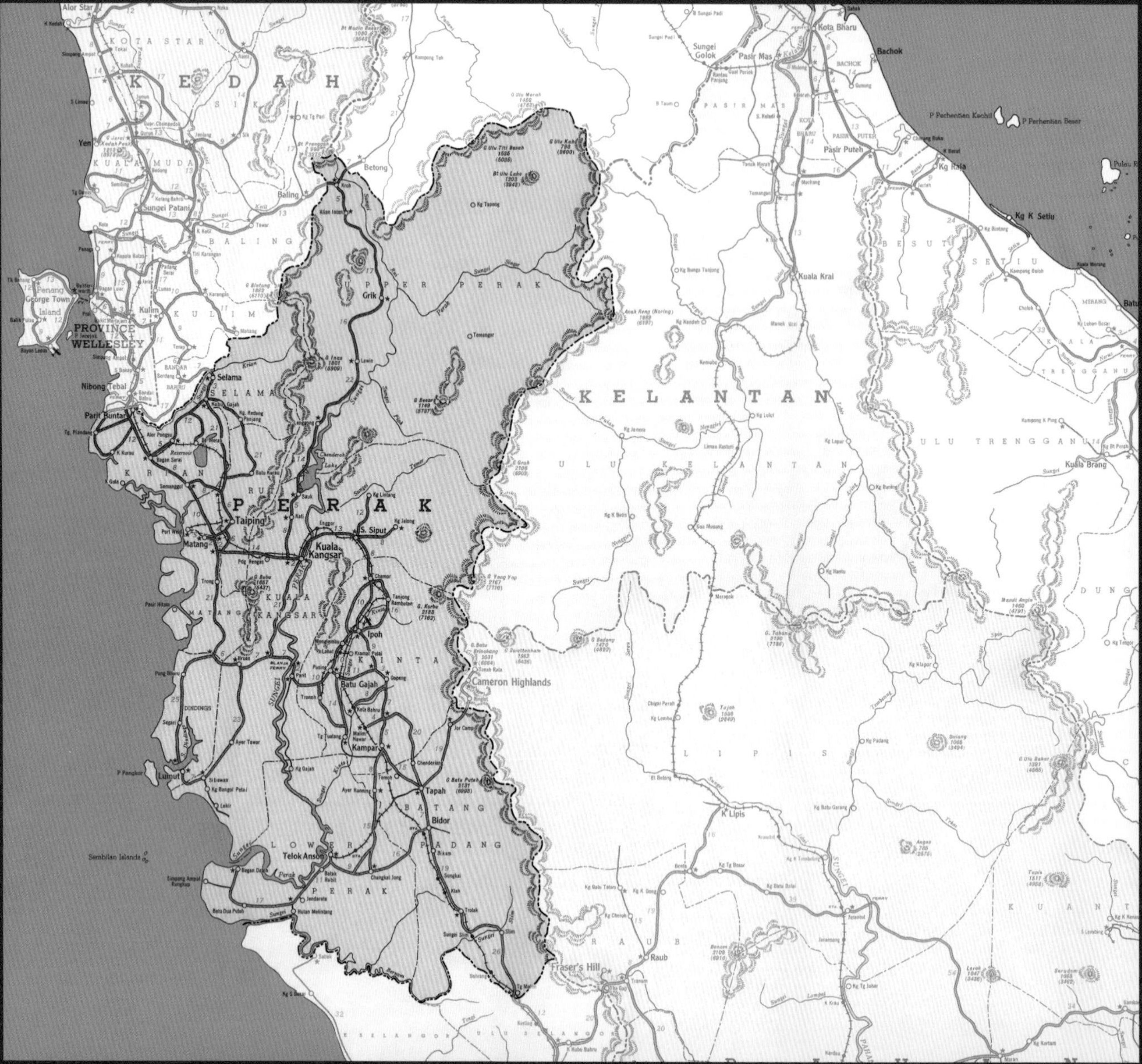

K E D A H
P E R A K
K E L A N T A N
PROVINCE WELLESLEY
Penang George Town Island
Alor Star
Yen
Sungei Patani
Kulim
Baling
Betong
Kota Bharu
Bachok
Pasir Mas
Sungei Golok
Pasir Puteh
Kuala Krai
Kg K Setiu
P Perhentian Kechil
P Perhentian Besar
Grik
Selama
Nibong Tebal
Parit Buntar
Taiping
Matang
Kuala Kangsar
S. Siput
Ipoh
Batu Gajah
Kampar
Tapah
Bidor
Telok Anson
Lumut
Cameron Highlands
Fraser's Hill
Raub
K Lipis
Kuala Brang
U L U   K E L A N T A N
U L U   T R E N G G A N U
L I P I S
Sembilan Islands

PERAK

Perak is the second-largest state in the Malay Peninsula. The name means "silver" in Malay, and was probably derived from the silvery colour of tin. The Arabic honorific name of Perak is Darul Ridzuan ("Land of Grace").

This was one of the richest states of the FMS, owing much of its financial wealth to its rich alluvial deposits of tin. From the late 1800s, tin-mining brought great prosperity to the state, which came to be regarded as one of the "jewels in the crown" of the British Empire.

The administrative capital of Perak is Ipoh, but Kuala Kangsar is the royal capital.

Kuala Kangsar: the Royal Town

The Sultan of Perak's official residence is in Kuala Kangsar (KK). Three past sultans are shown in [145–147]. [148] shows the Perak State Guard of the Sultan; its members were drawn from the Perak Armed Police which was formed in 1873.[26]

Two magnificent buildings dominate KK: the Sultan's Palace (Istana Iskandariah) and the Ubudiah Mosque [149–151]. Kuala Kangsar ("Mouth of the River of the Kangsar Tree") sits near the Perak River [153; 154]. Elephants were used widely in Perak for transport and ceremonial purposes [152]. An agri-horticultural show was held in KK [155;156] in around 1906.

The Malay College [157; 158] was established in Kuala Kangsar in 1905. It was set up as a boarding school to cater for the sons of the sultans and other Malay aristocrats; its students were exposed to western culture and Islamic studies. Many of the Agongs (Kings) of Malaysia have studied at this College.[27]

Ipoh: the Capital of Perak

Ipoh, the administrative capital of Perak, was built largely on the basis of the revenue derived from tin-mining [235–238]. Ipoh, in the words of historian Khoo Salma Nasution, "a pioneer tin-mining town in the late 1870s, became the meeting point of rivers, roads and railway, and the commercial centre of the Kinta Valley, the largest tin-producing region in the world." As she put it, the town was built by miners and migrants.[28]

Ipoh was named after the Ipoh (or Upas) Tree [160], a tall jungle tree from which the Orang Asli procured poison for the darts of their blowpipes.[30]

Two early views of the town are shown in [159]. The old Railway Station [161] was built in the late 1890s while the present Railway Station [162] was built in 1914–17; the War Memorial dedicated to the dead of the two World Wars [163] stands in front of the Railway Station. Other notable buildings in prewar Ipoh are shown in [164–169; 171–172].

The Kinta River divides the "old town" from the "new town" [170]; the two are connected by the Birch Bridge [173]. The most famous monument in Ipoh is the Birch Memorial [176–177], erected in memory of J.W.W. Birch, the first British Resident of Perak. The market, and some of the roads, streets and buildings of prewar Ipoh are shown in [175; 178–186]; also shown here are some schools [187–194], places of worship in and around the town [195–197], and a hot spring nearby [198].

Taiping: Town of Everlasting Peace

Taiping ("everlasting peace" in Mandarin) is situated north of Ipoh. It is a historic tin-mining town, and before Ipoh it was the administrative centre of Perak. It is blessed with extensive gardens and verdant hills.[33]

Founded in the 1870s, the town owes its existence to the Larut Wars. The town (formerly known as Larut) developed rapidly in the 19th century, after the discovery of tin. This led to an influx of settlers, mostly Chinese

The Sultan of Perak (most likely to be Sultan Idris I Murshidul Adzam Shah) is descending from the dais.
(*See* [147])

Treacher Street, now called Jalan Bijih Timah, was where many came to do their marketing.
(*See* [181])

The Perak Museum was established in 1883 in the former Government Office.
(*See* [204])

In 1897, the new Government Office building shown in this ppc was opened.
(*See* [207])

immigrants, who soon started feuding among themselves over the ownership of the tin mines. The feuds escalated into violent clashes (the Larut Wars) between rival groups. In 1873, the British, in a bid to quell the violence, appointed Captain T.C.S. Speedy to restore law and order. It was Speedy who eventually named the town Taiping.[33] A year later, the Pangkor Treaty of 1874 was signed.

While Taiping's early development was guided by Sir Hugh Low (Resident of Perak 1877–1889), it was Sir Frank Swettenham (Acting Resident of Perak 1884–1886) who developed Taiping more extensively.[26, 33]

An early view of the Taiping Railway Station is shown in **[199]**; **[200]** shows the Malay States Guides Barracks at the Main Road. Many of the town's other handsome and historic buildings are shown in **[201-209]**. The waterfall of Taiping and the Perak Club are shown in **[210-212]**.

The Taiping Lake Gardens **[213]** were opened in 1893. Originally a large area of abandoned tin mines, the site was drained, levelled and reshaped to form a beautiful garden.

Maxwell Hill and Bukit Pondu

Maxwell Hill (or Bukit Larut) **[214]** is Malaysia's oldest but least developed hill station resort. Developed in the 1880s to cater to British government servants, it was named after William E. Maxwell, the Assistant Resident of Perak. It is located 9 kilometres from Taiping and stands 1250 metres above sea level. Today, century-old bungalows such as "Tempines" and "Cedana" still function as guesthouses.[35]

According to *An Illustrated Guide to the Federated Malay States*, Bukit Pondu (or Gunung Pondok) **[215]** is a famous limestone hill situated between Taiping and Kuala Kangsar: "The railway passes through several tunnels to climb to the top of the Bukit Gantang pass... a fine view of Gunong Pondok and the valley of Perak beyond it."[32, 34]

Other towns in Perak

Surrounded by paddy fields, Bagan Serai ("lemon grass landing place") **[216]** is a small town at the border of Perak and Seberang Perai; the town was well-known for snipe shooting during the late 19th century.

In 1884, Batu Gajah ("Elephant Stone")[29] **[217-220]** was made the administrative headquarters of the Kinta district in Perak. After the discovery of tin, Kinta soon became the richest district in the FMS, and the Kinta land office in Batu Gajah became the most important land office in Malaya.[36]

Campar (or Kampar) **[221]**, named by its early settlers after their homes in Sumatra, is situated in the south of the Kinta district. The tin rush during the early 1900s transformed Kampar from the most backward mukim (sub-district) in Kinta into one of the more prosperous towns in Perak. Gopeng **[222; 223]** is situated south of Ipoh in the Kinta Valley. It was once the most important town in Kinta but was overtaken by Ipoh around 1890. Gopeng was the site of operations for many Chinese tin-mine owners, such as Chung Keng Kwee and Eu Tong Sen, as well as large European mining companies.[29]

Parit Buntar ("Buntar's Canal") **[227; 228]**, the headquarters of the Krian district, was developed during the late 1800s. Situated at the border of Perak and Seberang Perai, much of the land around the town has been used to cultivate rice, rubber, coconuts and sugar cane. Tanjung Malim ("the promontory of the religious leaders") is the location of Sultan Idris Training College **[224-226]** (now upgraded to become the Universiti Pendidikan Sultan Idris). Also shown are the Hot Springs at Tanjung Rambutan **[229]** and a Victoria Day celebration in Tapah **[230]**.

Telok Anson **[231-233]**, now renamed Teluk Intan ("Diamond Bay"), was named after Archibald Anson (Lieutenant-Governor of Penang, 1867–1877). The town's main claim to fame is its leaning clock tower **[231]** built in 1885 by a Chinese named Leong Choon Chong.

Other views

Elephants **[232]** were among the big game hunted in Perak; other game included wild pigs **[234]**, crocodiles and buffaloes.

[145]
Untitled [Sultan of Perak].

Cancellation: Nil
Back: Divided

A notation on the back reads: "Sultan of Perak". The figure in the ppc is likely to be Sultan Iskandar Shah II Kada-Shallah, who reigned from 1918 to 1938.

[146]
Untitled [Sultan Sir Yussuf II Izzuddin Shah].

Cancellation: Nil
Back: Divided

A real photograph ppc of the Sultan (c 1950); he reigned from 1948 to 1963.

[147]
H.H. The Sultan of Perak.

Cancellation: Nil
Back: Divided
Series and/or No.: 1074
Publisher: The Continental Stamp Company, Singapore

The Sultan (descending from the dais) is likely to be Sultan Idris I Murshidul Adzam Shah, who reigned from 1887 to 1916. Date: c 1910

[148]
Perak. Native States Guides.

Cancellation: 1911
Back: Divided
Publisher: Wilson & Co., Singapore

This sepia ppc shows the Sultan's ceremonial guards. Drawn from the Perak Armed Police, which was formed in 1873 after the Larut Wars, the guards consisted of a company of Sikhs and a British Commander.[26]

[149]
ASTANA ROAD, KUALA KANGSA.

Cancellation: Nil
Back: Divided
Publisher: A. Kaulfuss, Penang

This road leads to the Sultan's palace; a bullock cart and a rickshaw ply the road beside the river. Date: c 1910

[150]
THE NEW ISTANA. K. KANGSAR.

Cancellation: Nil
Back: Divided

This photographic ppc shows the Istana Iskandariah, which was built in the early 1930s for Sultan Iskandar. It was designed by John Craig Wilson of the Public Works Department.[12] Date: c 1935

[151]
Untitled [The Ubudiah Mosque in Kuala Kangsar].

Cancellation: 1921
Back: Divided

This photographic ppc shows the beautiful Mogul-style mosque and its domes and numerous minarets designed by A.B. Hubback.

[152]
Town View – Kualakangsa.

Cancellation: 1909
Back: Divided
Publisher: G.R. Lambert & Co. Ltd, Singapore

Three elephants are being watched by an admiring crowd in Kuala Kangsar.

[153]
Kuala Kangsar (Perak River).
Cancellation: Nil
Back: Divided
Series and/or No.: 166
Publisher: A. Kaulfuss, Penang

On the river bank is a houseboat (*left*) and people washing clothes (*right*). A buffalo is being washed in the river. Date: c 1920

[154]
Kuala Kangsar (Perak River).
Cancellation: 1912
Back: Divided
Series and/or No.: 173
Publisher: A. Kaulfuss, Penang

In the pcc is the railway bridge across the Perak River at Kuala Kangsar; on the river below is a houseboat.

[155]
KUALA KANGSAR A. SHOW WEAVING (SECTION: MALAY INDUSTRY).

Cancellation: Nil
Back: Divided
Series and/or No.: 152
Publisher: A. Kaulfuss, Penang

The ppc shows a weaving demonstration in progress, with an audience comprising many locals and two Europeans. Date: c 1906

[156]
KUALA KANGSAR. A. SHOW (SECTION: MALAY INDUSTRY).

Cancellation: Nil
Back: Divided
Series and/or No.: 151
Publisher: A. Kaulfuss, Penang

In the foreground of the ppc is a pair of large elephant tasks. There are house models and basketry in the background. Date: c 1906

[157]
"WHEELS" HOUSE. DEC.

Cancellation: Nil
Back: Divided
Publisher: Swan Photo Studio, Perak

On the back of this sepia ppc is a notation: "Malay College/Kuala Kangsar". The ppc shows a visiting dignitary posing for a group photo with students from "Wheels" House. The dignitary (with walking stick) is seated left of centre. Date: 1928

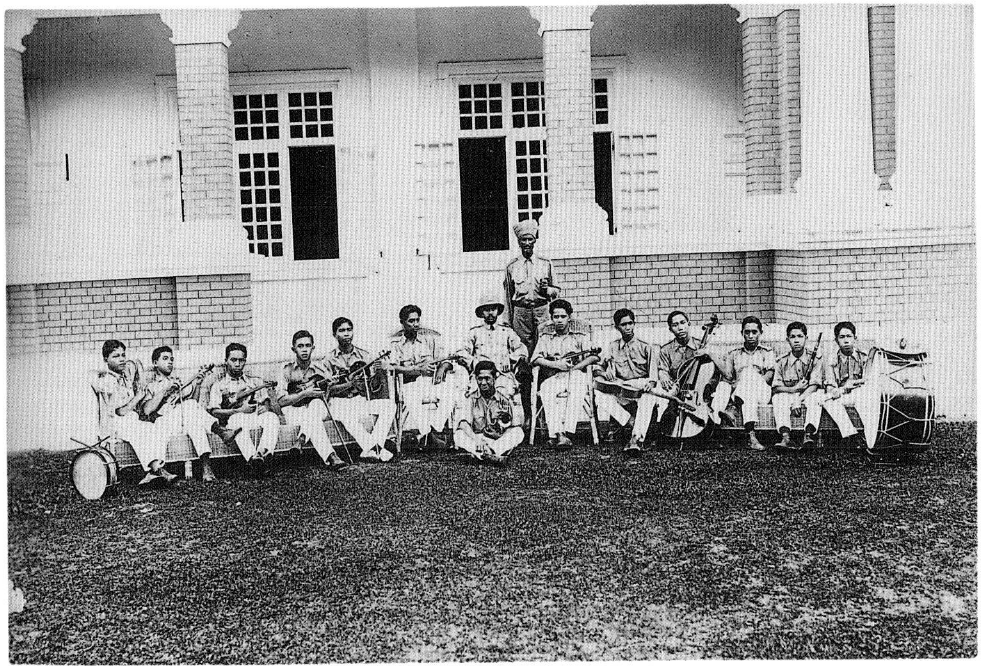

[158]
Untitled [Musical Ensemble, Malay College, Kuala Kangsar].

Cancellation: Nil
Back: Divided
Publisher: Swan Photo Studio, Perak

This sepia ppc shows the Musical Ensemble of the Malay College. Students of the college were exposed to western culture and knowledge.[27] Date: c 1928

[159]
Recreation Ground, Ipoh, Perak/Caves at Marble Quarries with Chinese Temple, Ipoh, Perak.

Cancellation: 1914
Back: Divided
Series and/or No.: 128
Publisher: The Federal Rubber Stamp Co., Kuala Lumpur

The Recreation Ground is along Club Road and faces the Royal Ipoh Club; the second view shows limestone caves.

[160]
Poison for the dart is furnished by the Ipoh Tree.

Cancellation: Nil
Back: Divided

This photographic ppc shows an Orang Asli harvesting resin from an Ipoh Tree. Date: c 1938

[161]
Ipoh Railway Station.

Cancellation: 1910
Back: Divided
Series and/or No.: 159
Publisher: A. Kaulfuss, Penang

The old Railway Station, constructed in the late 1890s, was a simple single-storey building.

[162]
Ipoh, F.M.S. Railway, Station and Hotel.

Cancellation: Nil
Back: Divided
Series and/or No.: 5116

This was one of the earliest grand buildings in Ipoh. It was completed in 1917 in the grand British "Raj" style and was designed by the Government Architect, A.B. Hubback, who had also designed the Kuala Lumpur Railway Station. Date: c 1920

[163]
WAR MEMORIAL IPOH.

Cancellation: 1930
Back: Divided
Series and/or No.: 10

The memorial was built in front of the Railway Station after the First World War to commemorate those who died in the war. After the Second World War, a marble slab was added to commemorate those who died during the second war. These were removed in recent years and replaced by a marble plaque that read: "Memorial to the Dead of the two World Wars".

[164]
GRAND HOTEL, IPOH.

Cancellation: Nil
Back: Divided
Series and/or No.: 230
Publisher: The Federal Rubber Stamp Co., Kuala Lumpur

The mansion was originally the residence of the Dato Panglima Kinta Wahab and his wife, Toh Puan Sharifah. The Grand Hotel was run by Armenian hoteliers during the 1910s. It was later renamed the Majestic Hotel.[31] Date: c 1910

[165]
RESIDENCY, IPOH.
Cancellation: Nil
Back: Divided
Series and/or No.: 162
Publisher: A. Kaulfuss, Penang

The Residency was the home of the British Resident; it was beside the Kinta River.
Date: c 1910

[166]
RESIDENCY. IPOH.
Cancellation: 1920
Back: Divided
Series and/or No.: The Georgetown Dispensary Series, No. 1
Publisher: The Georgetown Dispensary, Ipoh

A front view of the Residence of the British Resident of Perak in Ipoh; it was a single-storey building with a large lawn.

[167]
Ipoh, Post Office.

Cancellation: 1910
Back: Divided
Series and/or No.: 155
Publisher: A. Kaulfuss, Penang

Mail from Perak was recorded from the late 1870s; the post office in 1910 is shown in this ppc; notice the sign "Post & Telegraph Office" just above the ground floor.

[168]
Post Office, Ipoh.

Cancellation: Nil
Back: Divided
Series and/or No.: 4

This post office was built in the 1930s to replace the previous building.

[169]
SUPREME COURT, IPOH.
Cancellation: Nil
Back: Divided
Series and/or No.: 161
Publisher: A. Kaulfuss, Penang

Built in 1909, this Court House was demolished and replaced by a New High Court Building in 1928. It was situated on Club Road (Jalan Panglima Bukit Gantang Wahab). Date: c 1910

[170]
IPOH TOWN.
Cancellation: 1910
Back: Divided
Series and/or No.: 156
Publisher: A. Kaulfuss, Penang

By 1910, the old Ipoh Town was fairly well-developed. In the ppc, a lone rickshaw is in the foreground; rows of brick buildings are behind it.

[171]
IPOH CLUB.

Cancellation: 1909
Back: Divided
Series and/or No.: 157
Publisher: A. Kaulfuss, Penang

The Ipoh Club (now the Royal Ipoh Club) was founded in 1885, and is situated on Club Road. During the early 1900s, it was a simple single-storey wooden building with a thatched roof.

[172]
IPOH CLUB.

Cancellation: 1937
Back: Divided
Series and/or No.: 6

By 1937, the Ipoh Club had become a handsome two-storey building. On the Padang (*foreground*), a cricket game is in progress.

[173]
BIRCH BRIDGE, IPOH.

Cancellation: 1908
Back: Divided
Series and/or No.: Empire Series, 5

The bridge was named after J.W.W. Birch, the first Resident of Perak. Opened in 1907, the Birch Bridge over the Kinta River extended Brewster Road eastwards. It is now called the Sultan Idris Shah Bridge.

[174]
RACE COURSE, IPOH, PERAK.

Cancellation: Nil
Back: Divided
Series and/or No.: 158
Publisher: The Federal Rubber Stamp Co., Kuala Lumpur

The Perak Turf Club was founded in the late 1870s; the British Resident and the Sultan of Perak were Honorary members.[12] Date: 1909

[175]
STATION ROAD, IPOH, PERAK./
CENTRAL MARKET, IPOH, PERAK.

Cancellation: 1911
Back: Divided

This is an uncommon ppc with two views: Station Road (*top*) and the Central Market (*below*).

[176]
Untitled [The Birch Memorial].

Cancellation: 1926
Back: Divided
Publisher: The Federal Rubber Stamp Co., Kuala Lumpur

The Memorial was unveiled in 1909 and dedicated to J.W.W. Birch, who had been assassinated in 1875. It was erected at a cost of $25,000.[28]

[177]
BIRCH MEMORIAL. IPOH.

Cancellation: 1923
Back: Divided
Series and/or No.: The Georgetown Dispensary Series, No. 4
Publisher: The Georgetown Dispensary, Ipoh

Encompassing the tower midway up is a frieze of famous people.[28]

[178]
PANGLIMA ROAD, IPOH.

Cancellation: 1911
Back: Divided
Series and/or No.: 158
Publisher: A. Kaulfuss, Penang

The road is dominated by a carriage drawn by two bullocks; there were few cars in 1911.

[179]
BELFIELD STREET, IPOH.

Cancellation: 1926
Back: Divided
Series and/or No.: 13

On the back is written: "One of the principal streets of Ipoh." The signboards on the left include: "The Ipoh Provision Shop" and "The Season Store". Belfield Street is now called Jalan Sultan Yussuf.

[180]
HUGH LOW STREET, IPOH.

Cancellation: 1934
Back: Divided

The Street was named after Sir Hugh Low, Resident of Perak (1877–1889). This real photographic ppc shows rows of Chinese shophouses. Hugh Low Street has since been renamed Jalan Sultan Iskandar.

[181]
TREACHER STREET, IPOH.

Cancellation: 1911
Back: Divided
Series and/or No.: 165
Publisher: A. Kaulfuss, Penang

It appears to be a "marketing day", as evidenced by the many vendors, buyers, horse-drawn carriages and rickshaws. Treacher Street is now called Jalan Bijih Timah.

[182]
CLUB ROAD, IPOH.

Cancellation: 1920
Back: Divided
Series and/or No.: The Georgetown Dispensary Series, No. 40
Publisher: The Georgetown Dispensary, Ipoh

This road was under-utilised, as shown by the sole bicycle and pedestrians in the ppc. The road is now called Jalan Panglima Bukit Gantang Wahab.

[183]
THE ISIS THEATRE, IPOH.

Cancellation: Nil
Back: Divided

The Isis Theatre was built in 1932 (name visible at the front of the building); it was designed in an Art-Deco style. After the Second World War, it was renamed the Rex Theatre.[32] Date: c 1935

[184]
CHENG BOK BUILDING, IPOH.

Cancellation: Nil
Back: Divided

This handsome Art-Deco Building (in Brewster Road) was built in the early 1930s; it was named after Chua Cheng Bok, the founder of the motor firm, Cycle and Carriage. The ground floor of the building was occupied by Hutenbach & Sons Ltd (*left*) and William Jack Co. (*far right*). Date: c 1935

[185]
MERCANTILE BANK BUILDING, IPOH.

Cancellation: Nil
Back: Divided

This four-storey Art-Deco building embellished with flag poles, swags and cartouches was built for the Mercentile Bank. Guthrie & Co. had its office in the bank chambers.[28] This building still stands.

[186]
TIMES OF MALAYA BUILDING, IPOH.

Cancellation: Nil
Back: Divided

This sepia real photographic ppc of "The Times of Malaya Press Ltd" building was taken in Brewster Road. Date: c 1935

[187]
ANDERSON SCHOOL, IPOH.

Cancellation: 1919
Back: Divided
Series and/or No.: The Georgetown Dispensary Series, No. 2
Publisher: The Georgetown Dispensary, Ipoh

The Government-sponsored Anderson Primary School opened its doors in 1909, occupying an impressive building at Douglas Road.[28]

[188]
NEW ANDERSON SCHOOL, IPOH.

Cancellation: Nil
Back: Divided

The New Anderson School was built in 1931 at Ashby Road, as shown in the ppc. Date: c 1935

[189]
THE NEW ANDERSON SCHOOL HOSTEL, IPOH.
Cancellation: Nil
Back: Divided
Publisher: Mongram K Ltd
Date: c 1935

[190]
ST. MICHAEL'S SCHOOL, IPOH.
Cancellation: 1930
Back: Divided
Series and/or No.: 25

St Michael's Institution was set up by the La Salle Brothers in Ipoh in 1912. This building was erected in the 1920s in Clayton Road.

[191]
ANGLO-CHINESE GIRLS' SCHOOL, IPOH.

Cancellation: Nil
Back: Divided
Series and/or No.: 26

Founded in 1897, the girls' school was first started in a wing of the ACS boys' school. The building in the ppc was built in 1927 at Kampar Road and was called the Anglo-Chinese Girls' School.[28]
Date: c 1920

[192]
Untitled [Anglo-Chinese School].

Cancellation: 1923
Back: Divided

The first English school in Kinta was founded in 1895 by Rev. W.E. Horley of the American Methodist Episcopal Mission. The building in the ppc was erected in 1912 at Lahat Road, with further additions to the structure being made in 1938.[28]

[193]
IPOH. - CONVENT ORPHANAGE.
Cancellation: 1919
Back: Divided
All convent schools in Malaya doubled up as orphanages; the orphanage in Ipoh consisted a large building in the grounds of the Convent School in Brewster Road.

[194]
THE CONVENT, IPOH.
Cancellation: Nil
Back: Divided
Series and/or No.: Kunverjee Maljec Series, No. 6
Publisher: Kunverjee Maljec
The Convent of the Holy Infant Jesus was founded by Sister Prudence in 1907 and the Convent started out with only eight pupils. The finest feature in the Convent Complex was its front block – it had a façade of neo-Gothic arches with trefoil-shaped window openings (complete with timber shutters). It also housed a magnificent chapel.[28] Date: c 1930

[195]
MALAY MOSQUE. IPOH. PERAK.

Cancellation: Nil
Back: Divided
Series and/or No.: 175

In 1898, work started on this mosque, "a very substantial brick building put up by Dato Panglima Kinta Mohamed Yusof in memory of his principal wife who died in the same year".[28] Date: c 1930

[196]
METHODIST CHURCH, IPOH.

Cancellation: Nil
Back: Divided
Series and/or No.: The Georgetown Dispensary Series, No. 37
Publisher: The Georgetown Dispensary, Ipoh

A group photograph is being taken outside the church; visiting dignitaries were shaded by umbrellas. Date: c 1910

[197]
CHINESE TEMPLE, GOPENG ROAD, IPOH.

Cancellation: 1918
Back: Divided
Series and/or No.: 205
Publisher: A. Kaulfuss, Penang

The cave temples are more than a hundred years old. "Sam Poh Tong" is one of the oldest and most popular temples.

[198]
HOT SPRINGS, IPOH.

Cancellation: Nil
Back: Divided
Series and/or No.: 154
Publisher: A. Kaulfuss, Penang

This is the Tambung Hot Sprints, a 15-minute drive from Ipoh towards Tanjung Rambutan. Other hot springs in Perak are found in Sungkai, Pengkalan Hulu and Kampung Ulu Slim. Date: c 1910

[199]
Untitled [Taiping (Perak)].

Cancellation: 1907
Back: Undivided
Series and/or No.: 14 056

This early ppc shows a visiting dignitary inspecting a guard-of-honour contingent outside the Taiping Railway Station.

[200]
Untitled [Malay States Guides Barracks, Taiping].

Cancellation: 1906
Back: Undivided
Series and/or No.: 14 059

Built in the 1880s, this served as the headquarters of the Perak Armed Police (later called the Malay States Guides). Today, it is the most intact and historically important military complex of its kind in Malaysia.[33]

[201]
Untitled [Officers' Mess in Taiping].

Cancellation: 1912
Back: Divided
Series and/or No.: 14 053

The message written on the back of this ppc read: "The Mess Building was of pleasing design and contained expensive silver plates and souvenirs and relics dating back to the Battle of Waterloo".[33]

[202]
PARK & RESIDENCY, TAIPING.

Cancellation: 1913
Back: Divided
Series and/or No.: 170
Publisher: A. Kaulfuss, Penang

Situated in the grounds of the Taiping Lake Gardens, the Residency was built for the Assistant Resident stationed in Taiping. Today, this building houses the District Offices of Taiping.[26]

[203]
Taiping, Post & Telegraph Office.

Cancellation: 1908
Back: Divided
Series and/or No.: 177
Publisher: A. Kaulfuss, Penang

The first purpose-built Post and Telegraph Office in the FMS was built in 1884, replacing an earlier timber building. Early mail in Taiping was carried by a relay of runners and ponies.[26]

[204]
Perak Museum, Taiping.

Cancellation: 1910
Back: Divided
Series and/or No.: 126
Publisher: The Federal Rubber Stamp Co., Kuala Lumpur

The Perak Museum's first curator was Leonard Wray, who built up its much admired natural history and ethnological collections.[26]

[205]
GOVERNMENT OFFICE, TAIPING.

Cancellation: Nil
Back: Divided
Series and/or No.: 190
Publisher: A. Kaulfuss, Penang

This ppc (c 1912) shows the first Government Office building, which was established in 1883.[26]

[206]
P.W.D. OFFICE, TAIPING.

Cancellation: 1926
Back: Divided

The building in the previous card was later occupied by the Public Works Department (PWD). Behind it are two bungalows on a small hill.

[207]
PUBLIC OFFICES, TAIPING, PERAK.

Cancellation: 1918
Back: Divided
Series and/or No.: 127
Publisher: The Federal Rubber Stamp Co., Kuala Lumpur

The Government Office building opened in 1898 was well-designed, and housed the Council Chamber, Offices for the Secretariat, Treasury, Audit, Education and Forest Department. Today it is the premises of the Larut-Matang District Office.[26]

[208]
TAIPING, CENTRAL POLICE STATION.

Cancellation: 1911
Back: Divided
Series and/or No.: 178a
Publisher: A. Kaulfuss, Penang

This police station was located "at a point about equidistant from the Chinese theatre, the market and other much frequented places" in Kota Road.[26, 33]

[209]
POLICE STATION, TAIPING.

Cancellation: 1909
Back: Divided
Series and/or No.: 202
Publisher: A. Kaulfuss, Penang

The clock tower was added to the façade of the Central Police Station building some years later. The police station doubled as a fire station. Today this clock tower still stands and the building houses the office of the Taiping Tourist Association.[23]

[210]
WATER FALLS, TAIPING.

Cancellation: Unclear
Back: Divided
Series and/or No.: 9348

The waterfall on the outskirts of Taiping at the foot of Maxwell Hill was a favourite picnic spot for the residents of Taiping before the Second World War. Date: c 1930

[211]
PERAK CLUB TAIPING.

Cancellation: Nil
Back: Divided
Series and/or No.: 125
Publisher: The Federal Rubber Stamp Co., Kuala Lumpur

The Perak Club was established in 1881 for the exclusive use of Europeans and Eurasians (mainly military personnel).[23] Before the First World War, there were two clubs in Taiping: the Perak Club and the New Club (on the west and east side of the recreation ground respectively).[34] Date: c 1910

[212]
THE PARK, TAIPING-PERAK./THE PERAK CLUB./ GENERAL VIEW.

Cancellation: Nil
Back: Divided
Series and/or No.: 3
Publisher: A. Kaulfuss, Penang

An uncommon black-and-white ppc with three views of Taiping. Date: c 1910

[213]
Lake Gardens, Taiping.
Cancellation: 1912
Back: Divided
Series and/or No.: The Georgetown Dispensary Series, No. 46
Publisher: The Georgetown Dispensary, Ipoh

The Lake with its Japanese-style bridge is shown in this ppc; the playground is in the background.

[214]
Maxwell's Larut Hills.
Cancellation: 1917
Back: Divided
Series and/or No.: The Georgetown Dispensary Series, No. 47
Publisher: The Georgetown Dispensary, Ipoh

Maxwell's Hill was developed in the 1880s and named after W.E. Maxwell, an Assistant British Resident. It is Malaysia's oldest but least developed hill resort.

[215]
Bukit Pondu.

Cancellation: 1909
Back: Divided
Series and/or No.: 164
Publisher: A. Kaulfuss, Penang

Bukit Pondu (or Gunung Pondok) is a limestone hill situated between Taiping and Kuala Kangsar. In the ppc, the hill is pictured with a railway track; a labourer is pushing a railway cart with two European men sitting in it.

[216]
Bagan Serai.

Cancellation: Nil
Back: Divided
Series and/or No.: 174
Publisher: A. Kaulfuss, Penang

Here, the small town of Bagan Serai ("lemon-grass landing place") is shown with a single horse cart along the road. The British used to go to Bagan Serai to shoot snipe. Date: c 1910

[217]
GOVERNMENT OFFICES BATU GAJAH.
Cancellation: 1907
Back: Divided
Series and/or No.: 21
Publisher: A. Kaulfuss, Penang

The Land Office and the Court Buildings are depicted in this ppc; the large buildings reflect the important status of Batu Gajah as the administrative headquarters of the Kinta district in Perak.

[218]
BATU GAJAH.
Cancellation: 1911
Back: Divided
Series and/or No.: 171
Publisher: A. Kaulfuss, Penang

The ppc shows the Post and Telegraph Office in Batu Gajah. The first post office was established in 1886; this building was erected in 1903.

[219]
Batu Gaja race course.

Cancellation: 1907
Back: Divided
Series and/or No.: 20
Publisher: A. Kaulfuss, Penang

Wherever Englishmen settled in large numbers, there would invariably be a country club, a padang for cricket and a race course; Batu Gajah was no exception. The Kinta Gymkhana Club was founded in 1890 and race meetings were held in Batu Gajah.[16]

[220]
Batu Gajah.

Cancellation: Nil
Back: Divided
Series and/or No.: 182
Publisher: A. Kaulfuss, Penang

A parade and inspection of a Guard-of-Honour contingent is taking place (perhaps to celebrate the King's Birthday); the dignitary has arrived in a motor vehicle. Date: c 1910

[221]
GENERAL VIEW OF CAMPAR.
Cancellation: Nil
Back: Divided
Series and/or No.: 168
Publisher: A. Kaulfuss, Penang
This ppc shows a church-like structure on the left; the town is in the background, and Chinese men with queues are in the foreground.
Date: c 1910

[222]
GOPENG, SEEN FROM THE REST HOUSE.
Cancellation: Nil
Back: Divided
Series and/or No.: 203
Publisher: A. Kaulfuss, Penang
The long building in the foreground is the coolie line, still extant, in front of what is now the school field. The town is at the foot of the limestone hills seen in the background.
Date: c 1910

[223]
REST HOUSE, GAPENG.

Cancellation: Nil
Back: Divided
Series and/or No.: 23
Publisher: A. Kaulfuss, Penang

"Gopeng" is misspelt as "Gapeng". A horse carriage is waiting outside the rest house.
Date: c 1910

[224]
THE COLLEGE HALL. SULTAN IDRIS TRAINING COLLEGE.

Cancellation: Nil
Back: Divided
Series and/or No.: 2

This sepia ppc (with a serrated edge at the top) shows the Dining Room of the Sultan Idris Teachers' Training College at Tanjung Malim.
Date: c 1940

[225]
SULTAN IDRIS TRAINING COLLEGE./
FRONT VIEW OF COLLEGE.

Cancellation: Nil
Back: Divided
Series and/or No.: 1

The college has since been upgraded to a University (Universiti Pendidikan Sultan Idris). The ppc has a left serrated edge, which means it was detached from a ppc booklet. Date. c 1940

[226]
SULTAN IDRIS TRAINING COLLEGE. /
THE PRINCIPAL'S RESIDENCE.

Cancellation: Nil
Back: Divided
Series and/or No.: 5

This sepia ppc (with a left serrated border) shows the principal's residence, which looks impressive with its porch and tall windows. Date: c 1940

[227]
PARIT BUNTAR.

Cancellation: 1908
Back: Divided
Series and/or No.: 169
Publisher: A. Kaulfuss, Penang

The town is situated on a river not far from the sea. Sailing boats and steamships ferry goods to and from the other coastal towns and Penang.

[228]
PARIT BUNTAR STATION.

Cancellation: Nil
Back: Divided
Publisher: Pritchard & Co., London

The railway line connecting Ipoh to Prai was built in the 1890s; the train is pictured approaching the railway station. Date: c 1930

[229]
AYER HANGAT HOT SPRINGS, RAMBUTAN.

Cancellation: 1927
Back: Divided
Series and/or No.: 9139

Tanjung Rambutan ("The Promontory of the Rambutan Fruit Tree") was a thriving mining town in the 1900s. Beside the Hot Springs, it is best known for its Central Mental Hospital. The Hospital started in 1911 as the Federal Lunatic Asylum; today it is called Hospital Bahagia Ulu Kinta.[29]

[230]
SPORTS WITH THE NATIVES, VICTORIA DAY IN TAPAH.

Cancellation: 1907
Back: Divided
Series and/or No.: 24
Publisher: A. Kaulfuss, Penang

Tapah is named after the giant catfish; the town lies on the border of Perak. In this ppc, taken in the late 1890s, the locals are seen engaging in sporting activities with Europeans on the birthday of Queen Victoria.

[231]
CLOCK TOWER. TELUK ANSON.

Cancellation: Nil
Back: Divided

The tower was built in 1885 by a Chinese, Leong Choon Chong, and was used originally to store water. It stands at 25.5 m tall and seen from this angle, has a leftward diagonal slant. On the exterior, it appears to have eight levels but there are only three levels inside. Date: c 1910

[232]
TRAIN KNOCKED OVER BY ELEPHANTS, NEAR TELUK ANSON.

Cancellation: 1925
Back: Divided
Series and/or No.: J.J. Series

This is a dramatic picture of a train derailed by a wild elephant. The steam locomotive is shown in this ppc.

[233]
GENERAL VIEW, TELUK ANSON.

Cancellation: 1907
Back: Divided
Series and/or No.: 25
Publisher: A. Kaulfuss, Penang

Teluk Anson (now Teluk Intan) is the chief town and port of Lower Perak. Ships came in via Bagan Datoh to dock here. It had one of the earliest railway services in Malaya.

[234]
PIG-HUNTING.

Cancellation: Nil
Back: Divided
Series and/or No.: 207
Publisher: A. Kaulfuss, Penang

Four European hunters (with hats) are pictured with the carcasses of two wild pigs, which are being carried by native helpers. Date: c 1910

[235]
Tin Mining, Perak.

Cancellation: 1911
Back: Divided

This ppc shows a hydraulic tin mine. The European miners are wearing "topee" hats while the Chinese workers are wearing larger straw hats.

[236]
Tin Mining, Perak.

Cancellation: 1911
Back: Divided
Publisher: "Kronheim" Printers, London

A group of European, Chinese and Malay miners are standing beside a drilling platform.

[237]
OPEN CAST MINE, TEKKA VALLEY.
Cancellation: 1925
Back: Divided
Series and/or No.: 3114
The open cast tin mine in this ppc belonged to Towkay Eu Tong Sen.[16]

[238]
DREDGING FOR TIN IN KUMUNTING, PERAK.
Cancellation: Nil
Back: Divided
Publisher: The Federal Rubber Stamp Co., Kuala Lumpur
Kumunting (or Kamunting) was a rich tin mining town. The floating dredge in this ppc is likely to have been owned by Towkay Ng Choo Bee.[16]
Date: c 1930

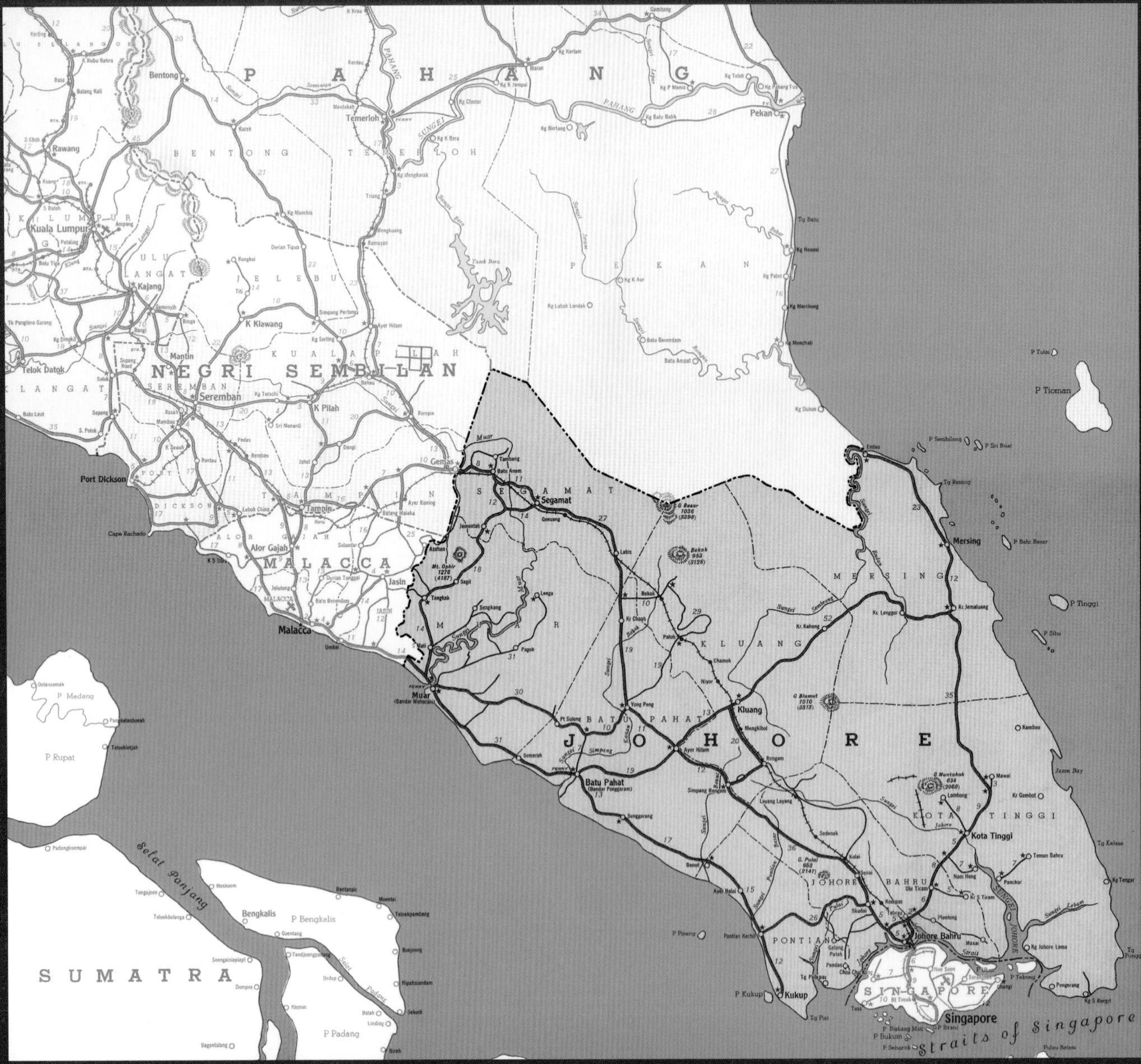
P A H A N G
Bentong
Temerloh
Pekan
Kuala Lumpur
Kajang
Rawang
Mantin
NEGRI SEMBILAN
Seremban
K Pilah
K Klawang
Telok Datok
Port Dickson
Gemas
Tampin
Alor Gajah
MALACCA
Malacca
Jasin
Segamat
Muar
Batu Pahat
Kluang
Mersing
J O H O R E
Kota Tinggi
Johore Bahru
Kukup
Singapore
SINGAPORE
P Tioman
P Rupat
P Bengkalis
Bengkalis
P Padang
S U M A T R A
Selat Panjang
Straits of Singapore

JOHORE

Johore (now spelt also as Johor), together with Kedah, Perlis, Kelantan and Trengganu, formed the Unfederated Malay States (UMS). According to the Anglo-Siamese Agreement (1902) and Treaty (1909), British Advisers were appointed to Perlis, Kedah and Kelantan (1909), and Trengganu (1918). In Johore, a General Adviser was appointed in 1909.[12]

Johore is named after its longest river, the Johore River. It is situated at the tip of the Malay Peninsula, at the most southern point of mainland Asia. Just to the south is the island of Singapore. The Johore-Singapore Causeway was built in 1924 to link Johore to Singapore.

The Arabic honorific of the state is Darul Takzim ("Abode of Dignity"). The capital and royal seat is Johore Bahru (the capital was previously Johore Lama).

Prewar, Johore was largely agricultural. However, most of the ppcs of that era feature either its capital or members of Johore Royalty.

The Sultans

Sultan Abu Bakar (1833–1895) [239] was the first sultan of modern Johore. He ascended the throne in 1862; on him were bestowed the titles of Maharaja (Emperor) and Sultan in 1868 and 1886 respectively. He had been born in Singapore and received a western education. This sultan came to be regarded as a man of wisdom, and was also a good friend of Queen Victoria, from whom he had received the above titles. In 1885, Johore signed a treaty with Britain, whereby the Sultan had to accept a British officer as his Adviser. Sultan Abu Bakar died in 1895 and was succeeded by his son, Ibrahim.

Sultan Ibrahim reigned from 1873 to 1959. He was featured in many ppcs [240–246]. Like his father, he loved "all things English", though in 1909 he had to accept a British Resident. However, he was compensated for this by being allowed to build up his own private army (the Askar Timbalan Setia). Unfortunately, as the colonial era drew to a close, his pro-British stance caused him later to be unpopular with United Malays National Organisation (UMNO) leaders, which led him to spend more time overseas, especially in Europe. He died in London in 1959, probably the longest-reigning Sultan in Malaysian history, having ruled for 64 years.

Sultan Ibrahim married four official wives who became Sultanahs of Johore. He is shown with one of his two European wives, Sultanah Helen, in [247; 248]. His successor (Sultan Ismail) conferred upon him the posthumous title "the Great".

Royal Palaces and Mausoleum

The Istana Besar [249; 251–256] was built for Sultan Abu Bakar in 1866 by Wong Ah Fook, a builder and entrepreneur.[41] It was a sprawling palace; the eastern portion was demolished in 1912 to make way for a banqueting hall. Shown in [254] is the "dining room" built in the "English Renaissance" style. In 1986, the palace was turned into the Royal Abu Bakar Museum after extensive restoration and renovation; it houses the many rare European, Japanese and Chinese antiques collected by Sultans Abu Bakar and Ibrahim.[38, 39]

The Bangunan Dato Jaafar [250 (*lower right*)] was built in 1893 for the first Mentri Besar of Johore, Dato Jaafar bin Muhamad (1885–1919).[38]

The Royal Mausoleum [257; 258] houses the remains of Sultan Abu Bakar in a magnificent monument. Though he had passed away in London, his remains were brought back to Johore Bahru, where he still lies close to his people.[37]

Sultan Ibrahim in his motor car.
(*See* [243])

The Bangunan Dato Jaafar.
(*See* [250])

A ppc with views of the Sultan Abu Bakar Mosque (*top*) and the Royal Palace (*below*). (*See* [267])

In the centre of the ppc is shown the main building of the Malay Training College; other views of the college are shown in the vignettes surrounding it. (*See* [289])

Johore Military Force

Before the Second World War, it had been the proud claim of Johore that it possessed one of the best equipped regiments in the British Empire. The Corps was initially founded by Sultan Abu Bakar in the 1880s to serve as his bodyguard unit. It was later expanded into an artillery company as well. Sultan Ibrahim took a very active interest in military affairs; he was the Colonel Commandant of the Johore Volunteer Forces and the Johore Volunteer Engineers.[37] Ppc [242] depicts Sultan Ibrahim in military uniform; Johore troops and the Johore Military Camp are shown in [259-262].

The Johore-Singapore Causeway

Prior to 1924, ferries [263] were used to transport people and goods from Johore Bahru across the Straits of Johore to Singapore. On 28 June 1924 Sir Laurence Guillemard (Governor, Straits Settlements, 1920–1927) declared the 1056-metres-long Johore-Singapore Causeway open. Sultan Ibrahim presided over the grand event. Initially the end of the causeway leading into Johore Bahru incorporated an electrically operated bridge-and-lock [266]. However, with increasing traffic, this feature was soon abandoned. Water pipelines were added at a later stage and still form part of Singapore's water supply.[40]

Johore Bahru

Johore Bahru (JB) is the capital of Johore. It is the southernmost city of mainland Asia. The town was originally named Tanjung Puteri; in 1886, Sultan Abu Bakar changed its name. Today, the sultan's name is perpetuated in many places in JB, including the Royal Abu Bakar Museum and the Sultan Abu Bakar Mosque [267 (*upper left*), 268].

During the early 1900s, JB was not well-developed [271-273; 298-299]; it owes its success to early Chinese settlers such Wong Ah Fook and Tan Hiok Nee, who contributed significantly to its growth.[42]

By 1909, railway facilities had reached JB [274]; the Johore Hotel is shown in [279]. Prewar travellers flocked to JB to patronise its gambling farms [275; 276]. *Twentieth Century Impressions of British Malaya*, published in 1908, describes "...the gambling saloons, in which a polygamous crowd may be met trying their luck at Chinese games *poh* and *fan-tan*. The attendance is especially numerous on Sundays."[16]

As one approaches JB along the causeway, a prominent building that comes immediately to sight is the Bangunan Sultan Ibrahim (Bangunan Bukit Timbalan) [269; 270]; the building was completed in 1941.[38] Some of the other public buildings in prewar JB are shown in [277-290].

Muar and Batu Pahat

Muar [291] (also referred to as Bandar Maharani) is a town in northwestern Johore. Its name originated from the Malay word *muara*, which means "estuary". The town is rich in history; it was founded by Lim Tong Lian, the leader of the Kang Chu clan of the Muar Straits. There were many gambier plantations in Muar in the early 1900s.

Batu Pahat [292] is situated to the west of Johore, on the Straits of Malacca at the mouth of the Batu Pahat River. Batu Pahat ("Carved Rock" in Malay) was a fishing town and distribution centre. To its northeast, iron was mined at Seri Medan from the 1900s to the 1970s.

Unique Johore ppcs

This range [253-254; 262; 272; 282; 293-298] of Johore ppcs is unique and not found in any other Malayan state. The picture is printed in sepia tone on a light cream-coloured card. On the picture side are embossed a blue star and crescent. Most of these ppcs are foxed with oxidised discoloration spots, probably caused by the acidity of the paper used. Many of these ppcs that still exist today are unused; those used were mainly from 1906 to 1909.

[239]
The Sultan Tuanku of Johore.
Cancellation: Nil
Back: Divided

A photographic ppc of Sultan Abu Bakar of Johore (1833–1895) taken in the early 1890s. He is in full regalia.

[240]
The Sultan of Johore.
Cancellation: Nil
Back: Divided

Sultan Ibrahim succeeded his father (Sultan Abu Bakar) in 1895. This is a photographic ppc of the young Sultan in full regalia. Date: c 1900

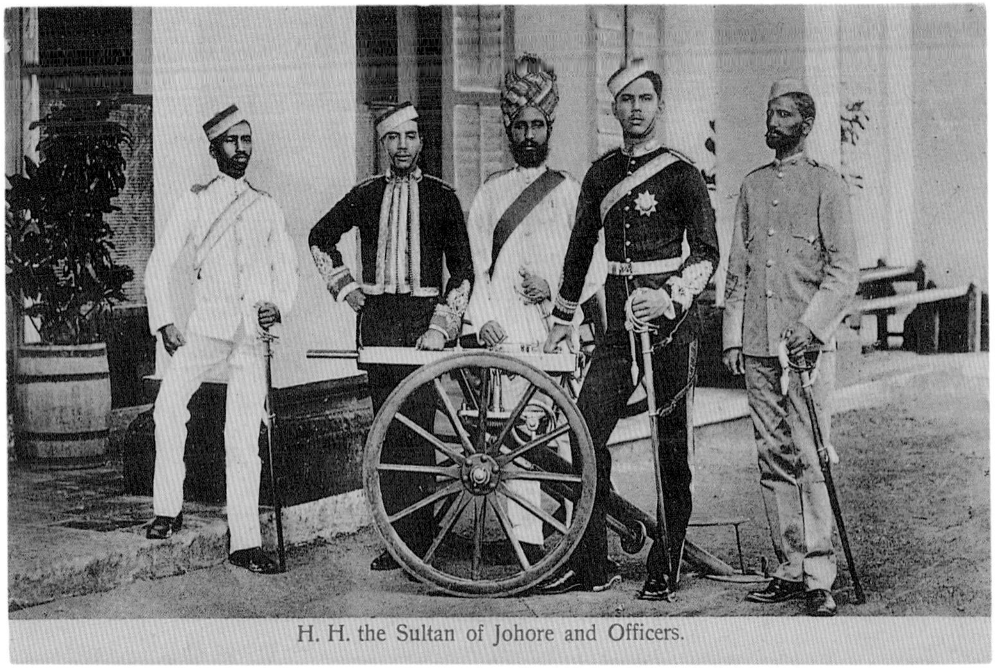

[241]
H.H. THE SULTAN OF JOHORE AND OFFICERS.

Cancellation: Nil
Back: Divided
Publisher: G.R. Lambert & Co. Ltd, Singapore

In this sepia ppc, the young Sultan Ibrahim (*second from right*) is posing beside a ceremonial cannon. Date: c 1900

[242]
H.H. THE SULTAN OF JOHORE AS COLONEL OF THE JOHORE FORCES AT KING'S BIRTHDAY PARADE IN SINGAPORE.

Cancellation: Nil
Back: Divided

Sultan Ibrahim was a great Anglophile; he took part regularly in the birthday parades of King Edward VII and George V. Date: c 1910

[243]
S. Ibrahim on his 120 H.P. Mercédés.

Cancellation: 1912
Back: Divided

Sultan Ibrahim was enthusiastic about cars and was one of the earliest car owners in Malaya.

[244]
His Highness The Sultan of Johor.

Cancellation: Nil
Back: Divided
Publisher: Johore Hotel, Johore Bahru

Sultan Ibrahim was a great hunter of big game. Here he is posing in his hunting gear with a tiger that he shot. Johore has been called "The Land of Tigers" and its Coat of Arms depicts a crown surmounting a shield supported by a pair of tigers.[37] Date: c 1920

[245]
HIS HIGHNESS THE SULTAN OF JOHORE.

Cancellation: 1908
Back: Divided
Publisher: Johore Hotel, Johore Bahru

A portrait of a young Sultan Ibrahim resplendent in full regalia.

[246]
JOHORE SULTAN.

Cancellation: Nil
Back: Divided
Series and/or No.: 333 849

Sultan Ibrahim loved horses. Here, as the Colonel Commandant of his Johore Forces, he is pictured on horseback. Date: c 1920

[247]
JOHORE STATE MALAY.
Cancellation: Nil
Back: Divided
Sultan Ibrahim posing with Sultanah Helen (Helen Bartholomew Wilson). Date: c 1930

[248]
Untitled [The Sultan and Sultanah of Johore].
Cancellation: Nil
Back: Divided
Sultan Ibrahim with Sultanah Helen at her coronation on 18 November 1931, at the Istana Besar in Johore Bahru.

[249]
JOHORE SULTAN RESIDENCE, JOHORE.
Cancellation: Nil
Back: Divided
Series and/or No.: 333 850
The Istana Besar, built in 1866 by Wong Ah Fook, a builder and entrepreneur.[41] Date: c 1910

[250]
SULTAN RESIDENCE, JOHORE.
Cancellation: Nil
Back: Divided
Series and/or No.: 1066
Publisher: The Continental Stamp Company, Singapore
This is the Bangunan Dato Jafaar – it was built in 1893 for the first Mentri Besar of Johore. It was modelled after Hardwick Hall in England. Its imposing square towers added to the grandeur of the Palladian-styled building.[38] Date: c 1910

[251]
INTERIOR OF THE SULTANS PALACE, JOHORE.

Cancellation: Nil
Back: Divided
Publisher: G.R. Lambert & Co. Ltd, Singapore

This is the Drawing Room of the Istana Besar, where beautiful Italian chandeliers hung from the ceiling, and rare Japanese and Chinese porcelain vases lined the walls. European furniture adorned the room. Date: c 1905

[252]
THE SULTAN'S PALACE, JOHORE.

Cancellation: Nil
Back: Divided
Publisher: Koh & Co., Singapore

The Istana Besar was completed two years before Sultan Abu Bakar was made Maharaja of Johore. This is a different view of the palace shown in [249]. Date: c 1910

[253]
THE THRONE ROOM. JOHORE ISTANA.

Cancellation: Nil
Back: Undivided
Publisher: State of Johore

The Throne Room at the Istana Besar with two beautifully carved golden thrones made by Johore craftsmen towards the end of the 19th century. Massive Italian chandeliers (which Sultan Ibrahim collected during his European trips) adorn the ceiling; an Italian marble sculpture is seen in the right foreground.
Date: c 1905

[254]
THE DINING ROOM, JOHORE ISTANA.

Cancellation: Nil
Back: Divided
Publisher: State of Johore

The Dining Room at the Istana Besar was famous for its magnificent Ellenborough gold dining set and central pieces which Sultan Ibrahim purchased in England. The ceiling has *punkah* fans.
Date: c 1912

[255]
GARDENS AT THE ISTANA – JOHORE.

Cancellation: Nil
Back: Divided
Publisher: G.R. Lambert & Co. Ltd, Singapore

The Istana Besar is surrounded by extensive gardens with many palm trees. Date: c 1910

[256]
ENTRANCE TO GARDENS, JOHORE.

Cancellation: Nil
Back: Divided
Series and/or No.: 1006
Publisher: The Continental Stamp Company, Singapore

This ppc shows the entrance to the garden besides the Istana Besar; a rickshaw sits idly by the roadside. Date: c 1910

[257]
THE LATE SULTAN'S GRAVE, JOHORE.

Cancellation: Nil
Back: Divided
Series and/or No.: 36
Publisher: Koh & Co., Singapore

The Royal Mausoleum of Sultan Abu Bakar (1833–1895) in Johore Bahru; it is one of the grandest in Malaysia. Date: c 1910

[258]
STONE MONUMET OF THE LATE SULTAN JOHORE BAHRU.

Cancellation: Nil
Back: Divided

A real photographic black-and-white ppc of the interior of the Royal Mausoleum of Sultan Abu Bakar. Date: c 1930

[259]
A COMPANY OF JOHORE TROOPS.
Cancellation: 1910
Back: Divided
Publisher: G.R. Lambert & Co. Ltd, Singapore
A company of Johore troops during a parade.

[260]
JOHORE SOLDIER'S.
Cancellation: Nil
Back: Divided
A group of Johore soldiers standing on a wooden wharf. Date: c 1930

[261]
THE VIEW OF MILITARY CAMP, JOHORE BARU.

Cancellation: Nil
Back: Divided
Publisher: T. Hamaguchi

The Military Camp was situated at Bukit Timbalan. Both Sultans Abu Bakar and Ibrahim took active interest in the development of the Military Forces in Johore. On 15 February 1915, Sultan Ibrahim led about 150 soldiers to help the British subdue the sepoy mutineers in Singapore.[37] Date: c 1900

[262]
SOUNDING THE REVEILLE, JOHORE.

Cancellation: Nil
Back: Undivided
Publisher: State of Johore

A sepia ppc showing a solider blowing the bugle; this was the morning wake-up call at the Military Camp at Bukit Timbalan. Date: c 1905

[263]
Untitled [Ferry of Johore].

Cancellation: Nil
Back: Divided

Prior to the completion of the Causeway in 1924, people and goods were ferried from Johore Bahru to Singapore by ferryboats. The roll-on railway tracks allowed train wagons to be ferried to Woodlands in Singapore. Date: c 1920

Causeway between Singapore Island and Johore

[264]
CAUSEWAY BETWEEN SINGAPORE ISLAND AND JOHORE.

Cancellation: Nil
Back: Divided

The Causeway is 1056 m long; it was officially opened on 28 June 1924 by Sir Laurence Guillemard, in the presence of Sultan Ibrahim. Date: c 1925

[265]
Causeway, Singapore–Johore.

Cancellation: Nil
Back: Divided
Series and/or No.: 23
Publisher: PYW

This ppc shows the Johore end of the Causeway. A bridge-and-lock is being lowered for a train (*right*) to cross from Johore to Singapore.
Date: c 1925

[266]
Lock Upon Johore Couseway.

Cancellation: Nil
Back: Divided

The movable section of the bridge-and-lock weighed 570 tons, the rolling lift of the bridge spanned the lock, thus being able to lift part of the railway and roadway. This feature was abandoned when the volume of traffic increased.[40]
Date: c 1925

[267]
Greetings from the Far East.
Cancellation: 1903
Back: Undivided
Publisher: G.R. Lambert & Co. Ltd, Singapore

A ppc with views of the Sultan Abu Bakar Mosque (*top*) and the Royal Palace (*below*). The mosque was built from 1892 to 1896 and named after Sultan Abu Bakar. It was modelled after the English baroque style, as can be seen by its ornamentations.[38]

[268]
Mosque of Johore./Inside of Mosque.
Cancellation: Nil
Back: Divided

A photographic ppc with two views (exterior and interior) of the Sultan Abu Bakar Mosque. It has a capacity of 2,500 and was designed by Tuan Haji Mohamad Arif.[38] Date: c 1930

[269]
Untitled [Coastline of JB viewed from the Causeway].

Cancellation: Nil
Back: Divided

Behind the many sailing vessels is the tower of the State Secretariat Building. The tower was designed by F.G. Darrington and completed by Palmer & Turner in 1941.[38] Date: c 1941

[270]
JOHORE GOVERNMENT OFFICE BLDG.

Cancellation: Nil
Back: Divided

Before the Second World War, this building was known as the State Secretariat Building; today it is known as the Bangunan Sultan Ibrahim. The steel-framed construction incorporated Moorish-Indian details.[38] Date: c 1941

[271]
JOHORE MAIN ROAD.
Cancellation: Nil
Back: Divided
Publisher: Koh & Co., Singapore

The main road in Johore Bahru during the early 1900s had few buildings. It was a coastal road and the sea is visible in the background.

[272]
THE MAIN STREET, JOHORE.
Cancellation: 1906
Back: Undivided
Publisher: State of Johore

The main street in Johore Bahru; only rickshaws can be seen on the street.

[273]
STREET IN JOHORE.

Cancellation: Nil
Back: Undivided

The street has a row of shophouses; a rickshaw and a pedestrian are the only signs of life in the ppc. Date: c 1900

[274]
JOHORE STATE RAILWAY STATION, JOHORE.

Cancellation: Nil
Back: Divided
Publisher: Koh & Co., Singapore

By 1909, the railway line from the north had reached Johore Bahru; the single-storey railway station is shown in this ppc.

[275]
JOHORE MONTECARLO (GAMBLING FARM).
Cancellation: Nil
Back: Divided
Series and/or No.: 40
Publisher: Koh & Co., Singapore

Proceeds from gambling and the sale of opium provided the prewar Government of Johore with substantial revenue. Date: c 1910

[276]
JOHORE GAMBLING FARM, JOHORE.
Cancellation: Nil
Back: Divided
Series and/or No.: 1008
Publisher: The Continental Stamps Company, Singapore

The Chinese mainly ran the gambling farms. In the pcc, the row of rickshaws waiting opposite the gambling den are probably waiting for customers. Date: c 1910

[277]
POST OFFICE, JOHORE.
Cancellation: 1908
Back: Divided
Publisher: Phototyped in Berlin

The first post office in Johore Bahru opened in 1884 and its first post-master was Howard E. Bentley. The post office functioned in this building until 1913.

[278]
POLICE STATION, JOHORE.
Cancellation: 1909
Back: Divided
Publisher: Phototyped in Berlin

Twenty years later in 1939, "the police force consists of a British Commissioner, 6 Assistant British Commissioners... 1,021 Malay non-commissioned officers, 197 Sikhs... Fortunately, Johore is comparatively free from serious crimes".[37]

[279]
JOHORE HOTEL, JOHORE.

Cancellation: Nil
Back: Divided
Publisher: Koh & Co., Singapore

This hotel on the main street in Johore Bahru was packed with patrons from Singapore, who visited the gambling farms nearby. Date: c 1910

[280]
THE COURT HOUSE AND THE POLICE STATION, JOHORE BARU.

Cancellation: Nil
Back: Divided
Publisher: T. Hamaguchi

The Court and Police Station were housed in a handsome two-storey building; outside the building is a pavilion (*right*). In the foreground is a timber yard. Date: c 1910

[281]
THE PRISDN, JOHORE BARU.

Cancellation: Nil
Back: Divided
Publisher: T. Hamaguchi

The Johore Bahru Prison was opened in 1883. It was designed by Sultan Abu Bakar – he had visited prisons in Shanghai and Osaka to study them. The buildings were built by Wong Ah Fook.[41] In 2005, the prison was relocated to Kluang. Date: c 1910

[282]
THE MARKET, JOHORE.

Cancellation: 1908
Back: Undivided
Publisher: State of Johore

This ppc shows the old market (completed in 1894) standing in the middle of the Sengget River.

[283]
JOHORE MARKET PLACE.
Cancellation: 1909
Back: Divided
Publisher: Hartwig & Co. Succ., Singapore

The old market standing in the middle of Sengget River was completed in 1894. Small boats could come into the river and unload their cargo on Jalan Sengget. This site has since been filled in. On it are now office blocks and carparks.

[284]
JOHORE MARKET.
Cancellation: 1909
Back: Divided
Publisher: Koh & Co., Singapore

Another view of the market shown in [283]; boats could sail up the Sengget River to load and unload goods.[41]

[285]
JOHORE SAW MILL.

Cancellation: 1909
Back: Divided
Publisher: Phototyped in Berlin

The sawmill is beside a river; boats ferry the timber to and from the mill.

[286]
THE GOVERNMENT CLUB, JOHORE BARU.

Cancellation: Nil
Back: Divided
Publisher: T. Hamaguchi

This azure-toned ppc shows the Government Club (likely to be the Johore Sports Club). Date: c 1910

[287]
Govt Hospital of Johore.

Cancellation: Nil
Back: Divided

This photographic ppc shows the wards of the General Hospital (it comprised single-storey wards that had high ceilings and wide windows, which minimised cross-infections). The hospital is now called Sultanah Aminah Hospital.
Date: c 1920

[288]
General Hospital Johore Bahru.

Cancellation: Nil
Back: Divided

The large flags (*right*) draped on the General Hospital probably meant this picture was taken in 1941–1942, during the Japanese bombardment of Johore.

[289]
Untitled [Five Views of the Malay Training College, Johore Bahru].

Cancellation: 1928
Back: Divided

In the centre of the ppc is shown the main building of the College; the refectory (*top left*); a classroom (*top right*); the dormitory (*bottom left*) and the front view (*bottom right*).

[290]
Untitled [Five views of schools in Johore].

Cancellation: 1929
Back: Divided

The words in fine print on the ppc read: "English College, Johore Bahru"; "English School, Batu Pahat" (*top left*); "Bukit Zaharah English School, Johore Bahru" (*top right*); and the "Convent, Johore Bahru" (*bottom right*).

[291]
Untitled [A view of the town of Muar].
Cancellation: Nil
Back: Divided
This ppc shows the town of Muar; the Muar River is to the right. A sailing ship (*centre*) is shown docked at the pier. Date: c 1910

[292]
Iron ore at Batu Pahat.
Cancellation: Unclear
Back: Divided
Iron was mined at Seri Medan to the northwest of the town. Here, around 1910, iron ore can be seen being loaded onto railway carts. During the Japanese Occupation, the Japanese kept the mines going for the benefit of the war effort.

[293]
PASIR PLANGI RUBBER PLANTATION, JOHORE.

Cancellation: Nil
Back: Undivided
Publisher: State of Johore

This ppc was published officially by the State of Johore. Such ppcs are identifiable by the blue star and crescent embossed at the top left hand corner; on its reverse side is printed the Johore Coat of Arms. Date: c 1905

[294]
THE PALACE, JOHORE.

Cancellation: Nil
Back: Undivided
Publisher: State of Johore

A view of the Palace complex from within the fort; the Straits of Johore is to the left.
Date: c 1905

[295]
Johore Sketches.
Cancellation: 1907
Back: Divided
There are seven views in this ppc; a rickshaw puller and his rickshaw in the centre are surrounded by four riverine scenes and two vignettes showing Indian snake charmers (*bottom left*) and Indian men with jars (*bottom right*).

[296]
Malay Boat, Johore.
Cancellation: Nil
Back: Divided
This ppc depicts a boat with two children inside; a wooden pier is on the right. Date: 1907

[297]
Awaiting a fare.
Cancellation: Nil
Back: Undivided
Publisher: State of Johore

A Chinese rickshaw puller holding a large straw hat is sitting on his rickshaw, probably waiting for customers. Date: c 1905

[298]
Views in Johore.
Cancellation: Nil
Back: Undivided
Publisher: State of Johore

This sepia ppc has four views: Johore Bahru town (*top*), Malay hawker and riverine scene (*centre*) and a rural scene (*bottom*). This ppc is unusual as it has four Chinese characters at its top left corner. Date: c 1905

[299]
Scudai Road Johore Bahru.

Cancellation: 1921
Back: Divided

Also known as Jalan Skudai, the road along the coast had tall Casuarina trees flanking it on the left, where the sea is also visible.

[300]
Johore.

Cancellation: Nil
Back: Divided

This ppc shows an arch built to celebrate a Johore royal occasion (perhaps the birthday of Sultan Ibrahim); the arch is decorated with a star and crescent surmounted by a crown. Date: c 1935

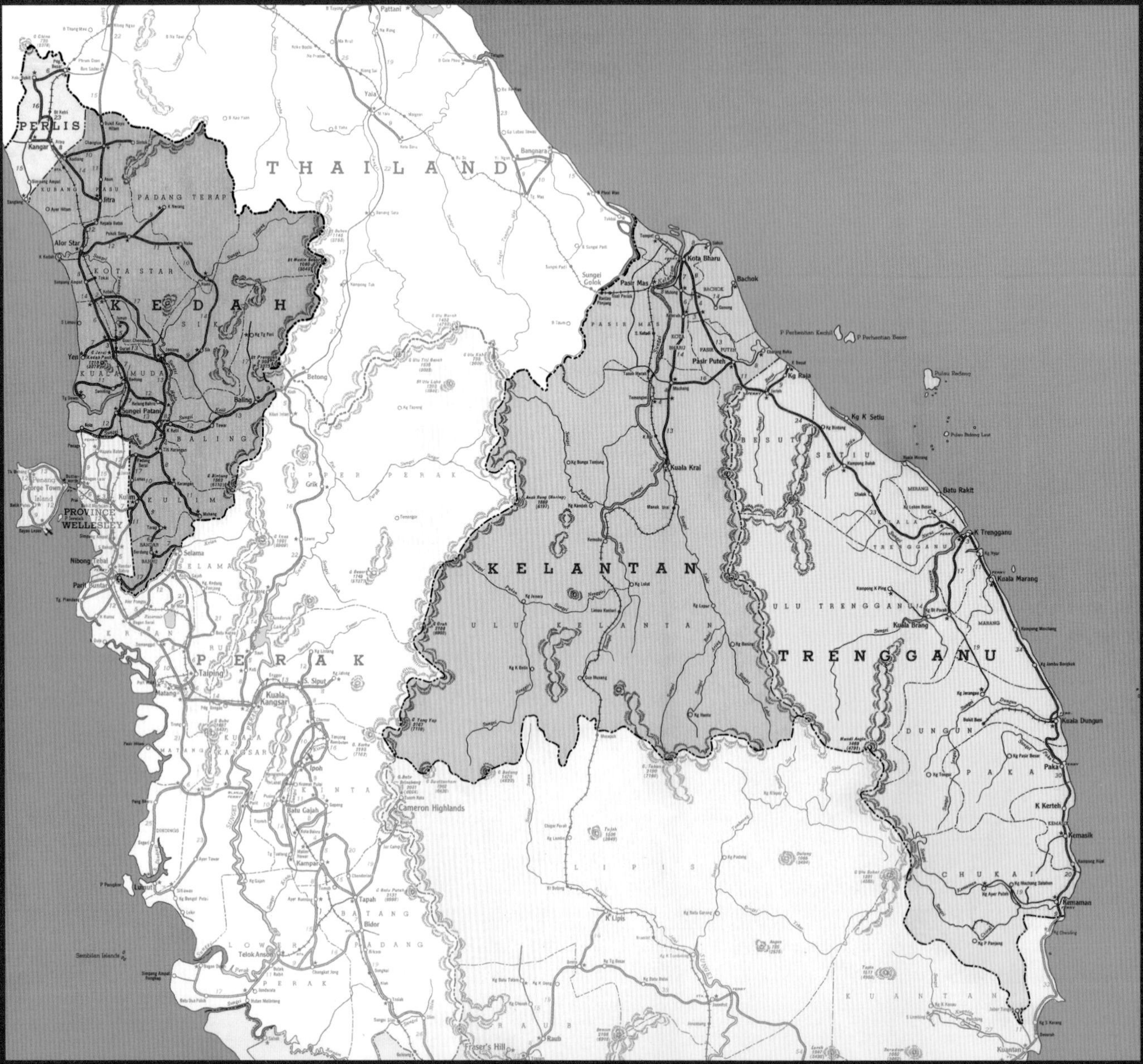
THAILAND
PERLIS
Kangar
KEDAH
Alor Star
KOTA STAR
Sungei Patani
BALING
Baling
Penang
George Town
PROVINCE WELLESLEY
Nibong Tebal
Parit Buntar
Betong
Grik
PERAK
Taiping
Kuala Kangsar
Ipoh
Batu Gajah
Kampar
Tapah
Bidor
Telok Anson
Lumut
Cameron Highlands
Fraser's Hill
Raub
K Lipis
Sungei Golok
Pasir Mas
Kota Bharu
Bachok
Pasir Puteh
Kg Raja
Kg K' Setlu
Kuala Krai
KELANTAN
ULU KELANTAN
K Trengganu
Batu Rakit
Kuala Marang
Kuala Brang
ULU TRENGGANU
TRENGGANU
Kuala Dungun
DUNGUN
Paka
K Kerteh
Kemasik
CHUKAI
Kemaman
KUANTAN
Kuantan
Pattani
Yala
Bangnara
Pulau Redang
P Perhentian Besar

KEDAH, PERLIS, KELANTAN and TRENGGANU

Kedah

The state of Kedah is in the northwestern part of the Malay Peninsula. The economy of the state is largely agricultural; hence Kedah together with Perlis is often called the "rice bowl" of Malaysia. The Arabic honorific of Kedah is Darul Aman ("Abode of Peace"). The proximity of Kedah to Thailand is reflected in its history, architecture, culture and cuisine.

Kedah has a long history; the Bujang Valley contains the remains of a Hindu-Buddhist kingdom dating back to the 4th century CE and therefore it is the oldest known civilisation in the Malay Peninsula. The current royal family can trace its line directly to this time. In the 17th century, Kedah was attacked by the Portuguese before being conquered by the Siamese in 1821. It remained under Siamese suzerainty until it was transferred to the British under the terms of the Anglo-Siamese Treaty of 1909. Kedah thus became part of the Unfederated Malay States, which it remained until 1948 when it joined the Federation of Malaya.

Sultan Abdul Hamid Halim Shah (1863–1943) [301–303] was the 28th Sultan of Kedah. He was the son of Sultan Ahmad Tajuddin III and Wan Hajar, and ruled from 1882 until his death. Tunku Abdul Rahman, who became the first prime minister of Malaysia, was the Sultan's 7th son and 20th child.

On 30 June 1937, a set of nine stamps bearing the portrait of Sultan Abdul Hamid Halim Shah was issued in Kedah. On that same day, an enterprising collector used one such stamp to frank and cancel ppcs that depicted the Sultan. Today, such ppcs are considered to be the earliest maximum ppcs of Malaya (a "maximum" ppc is franked with a postage stamp bearing a similar design [301; 302]).

Sultan Abdul Hamid Halim Shah had many children; he is pictured with two of his sons [303]. He had a beautiful country house [304], the Astana Anak Bukit, where he held lavish hunting parties with local chieftains and visiting dignitaries. It was (and still is) situated along the Mirban River (a tributary of the Merbok River)[44] and overlooked the Kedah peak (Gunung Jerai) near Gurun/Sungai Petani.

During the 1800s and 1900s, elephants were used in ceremonies, as beasts of burden and for wars [305–308]. They were also kept as pets in the palaces of the Sultans.

Alor Star

Alor Star is the capital and royal seat of Kedah. It was founded in 1735 by Kedah's 19th ruler, Sultan Muhammad Jiwa Zainal Abidin II. Alor Star has several buildings of historical interest, including the Balai Nobat [310–311], the Big Clock Tower [309], the Masjid Zahir [309; 312 (*upper right*)] and the Public Offices [313]. The Public Offices were built in 1893 and used for a variety of purposes until 1983, when the building was converted into the Balai Seni Negeri (State Art Gallery). The Wan Mat Saman Bridge [314] was opened on 14 July 1926; it crosses the Kedah River at the entrance to Alor Star. The Bridge consists of five arches with a total length of 85 metres.

The post office in Alor Star [315] was opened about 1907; the General Post Office [316] was built later. The Hong Kong and Shanghai Bank Building in Sungai Petani is shown in ppcs [317 (*lower right*); 318]. Located south of Alor Star, the town of Sungai Petani ("Farmer River" in Malay) was so named due to the large concentration of paddy fields [319; 320] and farms nearby.

The Masjid Zahir in Alor Star was built in 1912 on the site of a cemetery.
(*See* [312])

The Hong Kong and Shanghai Bank Building, Sungai Patani, which was designed in the Art-Deco style.
(*See* [317])

This sepia ppc shows two Malay men dancing to the music played by the three musicians. (*See* [333])

Tiger hunting was popular in prewar Malaya, as illustrated by this ppc of a hunter posing with his "game". (*See* [334])

Perlis

Perlis was the smallest and most northerly state of the Unfederated Malay States. It is bounded by Thailand in the north and by Kedah in the east and south. Its western coastline borders the Strait of Malacca; its state capital is Kangar but its royal capital is Arau.

No ppcs depicting prewar Perlis have been discovered so far; this could be attributed to its remote geographical location and lack of visitors before the Second World War. Of the few ppcs sent from Kangar in the 1930s, all had scenes showing either Penang or Singapore. The earliest ppc of Perlis (c 1945) in the author's collection shows Perlis's 6th Raja – Tuanku Syed Putra [322], who ruled from 1945 until his death in 2000.[65]

Kelantan

Located on the east coast of Malaysia, Kelantan is bordered to its north by Thailand. To its northeast is the South China Sea. The Arabic honorific of this state is Darul Naim ("The Beautiful Abode"). It is also known as the "Cradle of Malay Culture" and "The Land of Lightning". Kelantan is an agrarian state with lush rice fields, rustic fishing villages and beaches lined with casuarina trees.[66]

Prior to the Anglo-Siamese Treaty of 1909, Siam held suzerainty over Kelantan. As a result, Siamese postage stamps were used. Today, though Siam (now Thailand) has long since surrendered its claims to Kelantan, Siamese influence is still strong in the state, as can be seen in its architecture, cuisine and culture.

Dr John Gimlette was a medical officer in Malaya from 1896 to 1914; he spent ten years in this period working in Kelantan[67] as a residency surgeon of the Royal Army Medical Corps. It is speculated that he was also a medical adviser to the Duff Development Company (owned by R.W. Duff, a former British official in Pahang), a mining company which held a monopoly on mining rights in about one-third of Kelantan.[46] Dr Gimlette sent many ppcs from Kelantan to his sister (R. Gimlette) in Southsea, England; among these was one which showed a gold dredge belonging to the Duff Development Company [323]. This postcard is extremely rare. During the early 18th century, gold had been mined in Kelantan on a small-scale basis and it was no surprise that the Duff Development Company eventually closed down during the 1910s.

Kota Bharu is the state capital of Kelantan; it was founded by Sultan Muhammad II in 1844 and is the administrative centre for the state's bustling trade and cultural activities. The Muhammadi Mosque is shown in [325], while [326] shows the Market Square. Kota Bharu has a historic bridge, the Guillemard Railway Bridge, named after Sir Laurence Guillemard, Governor of the Straits Settlements (1920–1927). The bridge was completed in 1924; its construction is shown in [324].

Trengganu

Trengganu (today spelt Terengganu) is located on the east coast of the Malay Peninsula and was part of the Unfederated Malay States from 1909 to 1948. Its Arabic honorific name is Darul Iman ("Abode of Faith"). It comprises the basins of 12 rivers, all of which flow into the South China Sea. The longest is the Trengganu River, from which the state derived its name.[47] Originally a forested area, Trengganu was transformed during the mid-1970s, after the discovery of oil and gas offshore. It is now a popular tourist destination particularly for those interested in scuba diving and other sea sports.

Views of the Trengganu River and its harbour are shown in [327–329]. Other ppcs in the author's collection include: a gathering at the District Officer's house in Kemaman [330]; the Kemaman River [331]; a Malay House [332]; and Malay silat exponents [333 (*upper left*)].

Unfortunately, the tigers which roamed supreme in prewar Malaya were eventually hunted till near extinction in the states of Trengganu [334 (*lower left*)], Kelantan, Pahang and Perak.[48]

[301]
Untitled [The Sultan of Kedah].

Cancellation: 1937
Back: Divided

This ppc is a maximum card. Sultan Abdul Hamid Halim Shah is featured on both the ppc and the 10¢ postage stamp. The stamp was cancelled on the first day of its issue.

[302]
Untitled [The Sultan of Kedah].

Cancellation: 1937
Back: Divided
Publisher: Lai Chan, Alor Star

Sultan Abdul Hamid Halim Shah was the 28th Sultan of Kedah; he ruled from 1882 to 1943. This is also an early maximum card.

[303]
Untitled [Sultan Abdul Hamid Halim Shah].

Cancellation: Nil
Back: Divided

The Sultan had many children; he is shown in this ppc with two of his sons. Date: c 1937

[304]
Mirban River with Kedah Peak.

Cancellation: 1910
Back: Divided
Series and/or No.: 139
Publisher: A. Kaulfuss, Penang

This ppc shows the lavish country house, the Astana Anak Bukit, of the Sultan. The house was situated beside the Mirban River and overlooked the Kedah Peak. It was sited near Gurun/Sungai Petani. The Sultan hosted grand hunting parties there.

[305]
H.H. THE RAJAH MUDA AND TONGKOOS RETURNING TO KEDAH.

Cancellation: Nil
Back: Divided
Series and/or No.: 64

In this ppc, the Raja Muda (crown prince) is shown dressed in a tie, hat and boots. He was probably returning to Kedah from Siam with a convoy of elephants. Date: c 1900

[306]
PRINCE NECORN SAWAN PARIBATRÁS DEPARTURE FROM KEDAH.

Cancellation: 1901
Back: Undivided
Series and/or No.: 62
Publisher: A. Kaulfuss, Penang

The Siamese prince (seated on the tallest elephant) is returning to Siam from Kedah.

[307]
PENANG. THE ELEPHANT RACE IN KEDAH.

Cancellation: Nil
Back: Divided

The elephant race was in Kedah, not Penang. There are several European men in the foreground. Date: 1908

[308]
ELEPHANTS, KEDAH.

Cancellation: 1910
Back: Divided

Three European men are being transported on elephants with their local "drivers" (*mahouts*).

[309]
KEDAH CLOCK TOWER AND MOSQUE.

Cancellation: 1924
Back: Divided
Series and/or No.: 839

The Big Clock Tower (*right*) and the Zahir Mosque (*left*). Built in 1912, the Clock Tower is located at Jalan Putera; its architecture incorporates Islamic and Hindu elements.

[310]
THE SULTAN'S MUSIC HALL, ALOR STAR, KEDAH.

Cancellation: Nil
Back: Divided

The sole purpose of this 18 x 5 m three-tiered octagonal tower (the Balai Nobat) was to house all the royal musical instruments. It was built in 1912.

[311]
THE SULTAN'S MUSIC HALL, ALOR STAR, KEDAH.

Cancellation: Nil
Back: Divided
Series and/or No.: 9141

Another view of the Balai Nobat; the musical instruments kept here are used to play *nobat* music for royal occasions such as royal installations and weddings. Date: c 1930

[312]
Untitled [Masjid Zahir (Zahir State Mosque)].

Cancellation: Unclear
Back: Divided

This mosque was built in 1912 on the site of a cemetery of Kedah warriors who died while defending Kedah against the Siamese in 1821. The mosque was inspired by the Azizi Mosque in the Lankat town of North Sumatra. The domes are black. Date: 1930

[313]
GOVERNMENT OFFICES, ALOR STAR, KEDAH.

Cancellation: 1918
Back: Divided
Series and/or No.: 47
Publisher: The Federal Rubber Stamp Co., Kuala Lumpur

The building was built in 1893; it was initially used as the High Court. In 1904 it was used for the wedding of the Sultan's five princes and princesses. In 1912 it housed the treasury and the office of the British Adviser; in 1983 it became the State Art Gallery.

[314]
Untitled [Wan Mat Saman Bridge, Alor Star].

Cancellation: 1936
Back: Divided

The bridge (now an aqueduct) was constructed in 1926; the photograph shows the five spans – its central span is 24.4 m long and the bridge measures 85.3 m as a whole. It crossed the Kedah River at the entrance to Alor Star.

[315]
POSTOFFICE A. STAR.

Cancellation: 1922
Back: Divided

A real black-and-white photographic ppc of the old Post and Telegraphic Office in Alor Star. The post office was established in 1907.

[316]
Untitled [The General Post Office].

Cancellation: 1930
Back: Divided

The General Post Office Building in Alor Star was a handsome two-storey building built in the Art-Deco style. In front of it is a traffic policeman directing traffic at the street junction.

[317]
FRONT VIEW OF HONGKONG & SHANGHAI BANKING CORPORATION. SUNGEI PATANI.

Cancellation: 1926
Back: Divided
Series and/or No.: 2835

This black-and-white real photographic ppc shows the striking building of the bank built in the Art-Deco style with an Islamic dome and stylised minarets. It is sited at a street junction.

[318]
HONGKONG BANK S. PATANI.

Cancellation: 1928
Back: Divided

A side view of the bank and its tall columns, arched windows (on the top storey) and Islamic dome. The street in front is void of traffic.

[319]
BUFFALO IN THE PADDY FIELD.

Cancellation: Nil
Back: Divided
Publisher: G.R. Lambert & Co. Ltd, Singapore

In a Kedah countryside scene, a Malay rice farmer is using a water buffalo to till his paddy field. Date: c 1920

[320]
NATIVE WATER WHEEL WITH BAMBOO CUPS. RAISING WATER FROM RIVER TO RICE FIELDS.

Cancellation: Unclear
Back: Divided

The method of irrigating rice fields used by the Malay farmers since ancient times. Date: c 1930

[321]
SILVER JUBILEE CELEBRATION IN SG. PATANI.

Cancellation: Nil
Back: Divided

A large portrait of King George V and Queen Mary was erected along the main street of Sungai Petani in celebration of their Majesties' Silver Jubilee in 1935.

[322]
Untitled [The Sixth Raja of Perlis].

Cancellation: Nil
Back: Divided

Tuanku Syed Putra (1920–2000) was the 6th Raja of Perlis. He was also the 3rd Yang di-Pertuan Agong of Malaysia (1960–1965). This card dates from c 1945.

[323]
Untitled [D.D. Co. Gold Dredge].

Cancellation: 1905
Back: Divided

This rare photographic ppc shows the construction of one of the Duff Development Company's gold dredges in 1905. It was sent by Dr John D. Gimlette to his sister (R. Gimlette) in England.

[324]
KHOTA BHARU, KELANTAN. RAILWAYBRIDGE.

Cancellation: 1933
Back: Divided

This photographic ppc shows the Guillemard Railway Bridge during its construction period (1920–1924). It was named after Sir Laurence Guillemard, Governor of the Straits Settlements (1920–1927).

[325]
Untitled [The Muhammadi Mosque, Kota Bharu].

Cancellation: Nil
Back: Divided
Publisher: A.S.M.K. & Co., Singapore

The Muhammadi Mosque is located on Jalan Sultanah Zainab. It was built in 1922 by Sultan Ismail. Kelantan is also known as Serambi Mekah ("Verandah of Mecca"). Date: c 1940

[326]
Untitled [Kota Bharu New Market Square].

Cancellation: Nil
Back: Divided

This real photograph ppc shows Singapore Cold Storage on the right. The street is plied by rickshaws, bicycles and a few cars. Date: c 1940

[327]
Pelabohan Kuala Trengganu.

Cancellation: Nil
Back: Divided

This photographic ppc shows the Kuala Trengganu Harbour. The harbour buildings are in the foreground; many boats and *sampans* are in the wide river. Date: c 1930

[328]
Light House & G.P.O. K. Trengganu.

Cancellation: Nil
Back: Divided

This view dates from 1930 and is taken from the Trengganu River. The G.P.O. (General Post Office) was established in 1910.

[329]
Untitled [The Trengganu River].

Cancellation: 1936
Back: Divided

A real photographic ppc of the Trengganu River; a lone sailing boat is in the foreground.

[330]
Untitled [A gathering of Malays].

Cancellation: 1932
Back: Divided

This real photographic ppc shows many Malays at the District Officer's house in Kemaman for an unnamed function.

[331]
SUNGEI KEMAMAN (SIAMESE MALAY STATES).

Cancellation: 1900
Back: Divided
Series and/or No.: 150
Publisher: The Federal Rubber Stamp Co., Kuala Lumpur

The Sungai Kemaman (Kemaman River) is another major river in the southern end of Trengganu.

[332]
MALAY HOUSE. TRENGGANU.

Cancellation: 1927
Back: Undivided

This ppc depicts the house of a Malay chief; its roofs are made from attap.

[333]
MALAY DANCERS.
Cancellation: 1928
Back: Divided
Series and/or No.: 140
Publisher: M.S. Nakajima, Kuala Lumpur

This sepia ppc shows two Malay men performing silat to the music played by the three musicians.

[334]
TIGER HUNTING.
Cancellation: 1907
Back: Divided
Series and/or No.: 87
Publisher: A. Kaulfuss, Penang

A European hunter has just shot a Malayan tiger; behind the carcass are his four Malay helpers.

NEGRI SEMBILAN
MALACCA
Kuala Lumpur
Kajang
Telok Datok
Seremban
Mantin
K Klawang
K Pilah
Port Dickson
Cape Rachado
Tampin
Alor Gajah
Jasin
Malacca
Gemas
Segamat
Muar
(Bandar Maharani)
Batu Pahat
(Bandar Penggaram)
Kluang
Bengkalis
P Bengkalis
P Rupat
P Medang
Selat Panjang
Tasek Bera
Mt. Ophir
1276
(4187)
PEKAN
SEGAMAT
MUAR
BATU PAHAT
KLUANG
KUALA PILAH
JELEBU
ULU LANGAT
KLANGAT
SEREMBAN
PORT DICKSON
TAMPIN
ALOR GAJAH
JASIN
Rembau
Bahau
Rompin
Labis
Bekok
Yong Peng
Ayer Hitam
Tangkak
Pontian Kechil

MALACCA

Malacca (also known as Melaka) is the third-smallest state in Malaysia. It is located in the south of the Malay Peninsula, on the Strait of Malacca. The state's capital is Malacca Town. Although Malacca was originally a Malay Sultanate, the state has no sultan today. Instead the head of state is known as the Yang-di-Pertuan Negeri (or Governor).

Malacca, Penang and Singapore were constituent parts of the Straits Settlements (SS) from 1826 to 1946. Malacca was the oldest and largest member of the SS,[16] and has arguably the richest and longest history. However it is the least developed commercially.

The Sultanate of Malacca was founded by Parameswara (a Hindu prince from Palembang) in 1400. Parameswara had escaped the Majapahit conquest of Palembang by fleeing to Singapore, and then to Muar, Johore. In 1402 he settled in Malacca and converted to Islam after marrying a princess from Pasai. According to the *Malay Annals*, Parameswara, who declared himself King, observed a mouse deer outwit a dog under a Malacca tree. Taking this to be a good omen, he named the town "Malacca". Today, the mouse deer is part of Malacca's Coat of Arms.

The Portuguese in Malacca

In 1511, a fleet led by Alphonso d'Albuquerque, the Portuguese Viceroy of India, conquered Malacca; thus setting the tone for nearly 450 years of colonial rule under successive colonial masters.[12] In 1512, the Portuguese built a fortress at the foot of St Paul's Hill [336], near the mouth of the Malacca River. The fortress was named A Famosa ("The Famous") [335 (*upper right*)]. However, the Dutch and the British destroyed much of A Famosa. Today the Santiago Gate [337; 338] is all that remains of it. After the Dutch had captured Malacca from the Portuguese in 1641, the gate was repaired, and a panel with the Coat of Arms of the Dutch East India Company and its monogram "VOC" (Vereenigde Oost-Indie Companie) was added above the gate. St Paul's Church [339; 340] stands on top of St Paul's Hill. Built in 1521, it is now little more than a ruin, having been destroyed by the Dutch.

The Dutch area

After its conquest of Malacca, the Dutch built brick houses and a large administrative building, the Stadhuys ("Town Hall") [341 (*lower right*), 343], to house the Dutch governor and his staff. Christ Church [342] was built in 1741–53 to commemorate the centenary of Dutch occupation of Malacca. Originally part of the Dutch Reformed Church, Christ Church became an Anglican church when the British unofficially took control of Malacca in 1795. It was officially consecrated for Anglican use in 1838.[49]

British Malacca

In 1824, with the signing of the Anglo-Dutch Treaty, the British exchanged Bencoolen for Malacca, and Malacca came under British control. British rule eventually ended in 1957. However, much of the British colonial legacy is still visible in Malacca today, the most prominent being the Queen Victoria Fountain [342; 346]. The fountain was erected in the centre of the Dutch Square in 1905 in memory of Queen Victoria, whose profile can be seen on all of its four sides. The Tan Beng Swee Clock Tower [346] was built in 1886; its clock-face was imported from England. The clock was replaced with a Japanese one in 1982.[49]

Ppc [344] shows the Malacca Rest House. As in other towns in Malaya, the British built rest houses (small hotels) for its officials to stay in while on their travels.

A Famosa stood on a small hill overlooking the sea and surrounding areas.
(*See* [335])

Constructed in 1650, the Stadhuys was designed in a Dutch architectural style.
(*See* [341])

The Tan Kim Seng Bridge was decorated to celebrate the coronation of King Edward VII. (*See* [352])

Fishing was a common activity for the Malays in prewar Malacca. (*See* [370])

There were three such rest houses in Malacca – one at Bandar Hilir, another at the Railway Station, and the last one by the sea at Tanjung Kling.[50]

The Malacca Club [347; 348] was founded around 1900 and it was the social focus of Malacca's European community; it combined the facilities of both a sporting and a social institution. In 1908, its president was the Honorable Mr Evans, the Resident Councillor.[16] Architecturally, the building is an eclectic mix of the bungalow form, Islamic domes and European columns and pilasters.[19] The Malacca Medical Mission [349] and Volunteer Drill Hall [350] are two other buildings that remain from the British colonial era.

Important events in Britain were also celebrated in her colonies. When King Edward VII was crowned in 1901, the event was celebrated enthusiastically in Malacca [351; 352 (*upper left*)].

The Malacca River and Sea

The Malacca River [345; 353-358] divides Malacca into two halves: on the east bank was the older European precinct (on which public buildings like the Stadhuys and A Famosa were located); on the west bank were business quarters as well as most of Malacca's Asian population.[10]

The Malacca River had given rise to a thriving port during the days of the Malacca Sultanate. However, silting soon made the port unusable. In [359; 360], the Pier and Harbour of Malacca are shown. By the time Malacca had become part of the Straits Settlements, it had already been overtaken commercially by Penang and Singapore.[10] The old town of Malacca and its seashore are shown in [361; 362].

Malacca's old Chinatown

Goldsmith Street and Temple Street were dubbed "The Street of Harmony" [363].[49] Along Temple Street, houses of worship stand side-by-side; the Kampung Kling Mosque is sandwiched between the Cheng Hoon Teng Temple and the Temple of Sri Poyyatha Vinayagar Moorthi. The Cheng Hoon Teng Temple (also known as the Green Clouds Temple) is the oldest functioning temple in Malaysia and was founded in 1645 by Kapitan Cina Lee Wei King.[49] The Kampung Kling Mosque was built in 1745; its architecture is Sumatran.[51] It has a three-tiered roof rising like a pyramid and the minaret is structured like a pagoda. The Sri Poyyatha Vinayagar Moorthi was built in 1781 and is under the joint management of the Malacca Chitty and Chettiar communities.[49] Ppcs [364-366] show the Kampung Hulu Mosque, St Peter's Church and St Francis Xavier Church respectively in Goldsmith and Temple Streets.

Multiracial Malacca

In Jonker Street [367] lived many affluent Chinese, especially the Straits-born Chinese (also known as the Chinese Peranakans). The Peranakans held elaborate and expansive weddings [368]. In prewar Malacca, Malays [369] mostly worked as fishermen [370 (*lower left*)] or as rice cultivators [371], while Indians were often found working in the cattle industry [372].

During the colonial era, many European missionaries came to Malaya to establish schools and hospitals. The Dames de St-Maur [373], which was run by Catholic nuns, was opened in Malacca in 1852.[54] Ppc [374] shows a British man with his car, driver and servant.

Outside Malacca Town

This survey of the prewar ppcs of Malacca ends with two towns nearby: Tampin [375] and Tanjung Bruas [376]. Tampin is 30 kilometres north of Malacca. Railway tracks led from Tampin to Malacca before the Japanese Occupation, but these were looted by the Japanese for the construction of the infamous Siam–Burma Railway (the "Death Railway"). The railway line was never rebuilt after the war.

[335]
FLAG' STAFF & OLD FORTRESS–MALACCA.

Cancellation: Nil
Back: Divided
Series and/or No.: 86
Publisher: A. Kaulfuss, Penang

At the foot of A Famosa were the government buildings. In the foreground was the pier.
Date: c 1910

[336]
FLAG STAFF, ST. PAULS HILL, MALACCA.

Cancellation: 1922
Back: Divided
Publisher: Wilson, Malacca

The flagstaff flies the Union Jack at its top; behind it lie the ruins of St Paul's Church.

[337]
OLD FORT, MALACCA.

Cancellation: Nil
Back: Divided

After the Portuguese conquered Malacca, they built a fortress (A Famosa; Portuguese for "The Famous") at the foot of St Paul's Hill. It was subsequently destroyed by the Dutch. Today all that remains is the Santiago Gate (shown in ppc). Date: c 1910

[338]
COAT OF ARMS. OLD FORT GATE. MALACCA.

Cancellation: Nil
Back: Divided

The Dutch captured Malacca from the Portuguese in 1641. They renovated the Santiago Gate; at its top was placed a plaster relief of the Coat of Arms of the Dutch United East India Company.

[339]
VIEW OF ST. PAUL'S FROM THE PIER, MALACCA.

Cancellation: Nil
Back: Divided

St Paul's Church was built upon the site of a former chapel built in 1521 by Duarte Coelho, the founder of Cochin China (India). He dedicated it to "Our Lady of the Hill" for what he regarded as his miraculous escape from the corsair attack in the South China Sea.[49]

[340]
CHANCEL OF ST. PAUL'S, MALACCA.

Cancellation: Nil
Back: Divided
Series and/or No.: 3

St Paul's Church was a place of worship for the Catholics in the 16th century. When the Dutch conquered Malacca, they destroyed the church. This bromide photographic ppc shows the chancel (near the altar) of the church. Date: c 1930

[341]
MALACCA.

Cancellation: 1906
Back: Divided
Series and/or No.: 96
Publisher: A. Kaulfuss, Penang

This ppc shows the Dutch Square with the Stadhuys (Town Hall) on the right, and the Christ Church (*centre right*) and the Tan Beng Swee Clock Tower (*centre left*).

[342]
QUEEN VICTORIA MEMORIAL FOUNTAIN, MALACCA, STRAITS SETTLEMENTS.

Cancellation: Nil
Back: Divided
Series and/or No.: 166
Publisher: The Federal Rubber Stamp Co., Kuala Lumpur

The Queen Victoria Memorial Fountain is in the centre of Dutch Square; the Stadhuys is to the right of the fountain while Christ Church is behind it. Date: c 1910

[343]
THE STADT HOUSE, MALACCA.

Cancellation: Nil
Back: Divided

This is a view of the Stadhuys taken from the pier in c 1920. There is a long line of cars waiting beside the building. In 1982, the Stadhuys was redeveloped into the Malacca Historical Museum.

[344]
THE MALACCA REST HOUSE.

Cancellation: Nil
Back: Divided
Series and/or No.: 13

This bromide photographic ppc (c 1930) shows the Rest House at the Railway Station. However, the station was destroyed during the Second World War, and its railway tracks were looted by the Japanese.

[345]
Untitled [Malaya. Malacca River].

Cancellation: Nil
Back: Divided
Publisher: Raphael Tuck & Sons Ltd, London

This ppc depicts a painting of the Malacca River. Coolies are loading and unloading goods from the Chinese junks moored along the river bank. Date: c 1920

[346]
VICTORIA MONUMENT & CLOCK TOWER. MALACCA.

Cancellation: Nil
Back: Divided
Publisher: Wilson, Malacca

The plaque on the Queen Victoria Fountain reads: "Victoria Regina 1837–1901. Erected by the people of Malacca in memory of a Great Queen". To the left is the Tan Beng Swee Clock Tower. Date: c 1930

[347]
THE NEW MALACCA CLUB, MALACCA.

Cancellation: 1914
Back: Divided
Publisher: Seikaido Muromanchi, Tokyo

The Malacca Club was founded around 1900; it was the principal rendezvous for the Europeans. It functioned as a social and sporting club.

[348]
MALACCA CLUB, MALACCA.

Cancellation: Nil
Back: Divided

This building was built in the 1920s to replace an earlier one [344]. On 31 August 1957, Tunku Abdul Rahman stood in front of this club to proclaim Malaya's Independence. Today, this place is known as the Proclamation of Independence Memorial.

[349]
MEDICAL MISSION, MALACCA, S.S.

Cancellation: Nil
Back: Divided
Publisher: C. Ishii, Malacca

This Medical Mission is likely to have been run by the British Missionary Society (London Missionary Society). Date: c 1910

[350]
MALACCA VOLUNTEER DRILL HALL.

Cancellation: Nil
Back: Divided
Publisher: Wilson, Malacca

This bromide real photographic ppc shows the Volunteer Drill Hall in Malacca. The signboard in the left foreground reads: "S.S.V.F. Headquarters/ Malacca Volunteer Camp". Date: c 1930

[351]
MALAY DANCING GIRLS, CORONATION DAY, MALACCA.

Cancellation: 1915
Back: Divided

The dancing Malay girls wore elaborate costumes; behind them a Union Jack can be seen; the banner above it reads: "MCDL DEPT". The photograph was taken during the Coronation Day of King Edward VII in 1901.

[352]
KING'S CORONATION DAY, MALACCA.

Cancellation: 1928
Back: Divided
Publisher: International Collectors Exchange, Malacca

The Tan Kim Seng Bridge was decorated for the coronation of King Edward VII in 1901. An arch was erected at the entrance to the bridge. Although the photograph was taken in 1901, the ppc was published later and was posted in 1928.

[353]
QUAY OF MALACCA.

Cancellation: Nil
Back: Divided

The Malacca River was crowded with *sampans, tongkangs, prahus* and *koleks*. On the left are landing steps for the loading and unloading of goods. Date: c 1920

ST. FRANCIES ZAVIER CHURCH. MALACCA.

[354]
ST. FRANCIES ZAVIER CHURCH. MALACCA.

Cancellation: Nil
Back: Divided

The Tan Kim Seng Bridge connected the two sides of the Malacca River. In the background are the twin towers of the St Francis Xavier Church. Date: c 1920

[355]
KIM SENG BRIDGE, MALACCA, S.S.

Cancellation: 1935
Back: Divided

The Bridge was donated by Tan Kim Seng (1805–1864), who also donated the Bukit Jelutong Cemetery and the Tan Beng Swee Clock Tower.[49]

[356]
LANDING PLACE SOUTH SIDE OF RIVER MALACCA.

Cancellation: Nil
Back: Divided

On the Malacca River is a large two-mast sailing boat. Other smaller boats are around it. By the river's bank is a row of two-storey shophouses. Date: c 1920

[357]
Landing Place, Malacca.

Cancellation: Nil
Back: Divided

This ppc shows the mouth of the Malacca River; on this site is now built the Malacca Maritime Museum (a replica of the *Flor de la Mar*, the flagship of the Portuguese fleet of 1511 that captured Malacca). Date: c 1920

[358]
Landing Steps Malacca.

Cancellation: 1923
Back: Divided
Publisher: International Collectors Exchange, Malacca

The landing steps on the bank of the Malacca River; in the foreground is a sailing boat manned by Indian sailors.

[359]
THE PIER AND HARBOUR OF MALACCA.

Cancellation: 1916
Back: Divided

Silting was a serious problem; this pier was extended further in order for it to reach deeper waters.

[360]
MALACCA PIER.

Cancellation: Nil
Back: Divided
Series and/or No.: 10

This bromide photographic ppc shows the long pier; ships using the Malacca port had to anchor at least two miles out to sea as the Malacca River was clogged by sandbanks.[10] Date: c 1930

[361]
OLD TOWN MALACCA.

Cancellation: Nil
Back: Divided
Series and/or No.: 185
Publisher: A. Kaulfuss, Penang

"When approaching Malacca from the open sea, one is impressed by its quaint and picturesque appearance... houses which face the main street have their backs to the shore."[16] Date: c 1910

[362]
THE SEA-SHORE, MALACCA. MALAY BOYS ROWING BOATS.

Cancellation: Nil
Back: Divided
Series and/or No.: 14

A bromide photographic ppc showing the seashore that is lined with coconut trees; Malay boys are rowing in two *sampans* in the sea. Date: c 1930

[363]
TEMPLE STREET, MALACCA.

Cancellation: Nil
Back: Divided

Temple Street (Jalan To'Kong) in Malacca's old Chinatown is aptly named. In the foreground is the Sri Poyyatha Vinayagar Moorthi Temple; in the centre is the Kampung Kling Mosque, and just visible beyond is the Cheng Hoon Teng (the oldest functioning Chinese temple in Malaysia). Date: c 1930

[364]
THE MALAY MOSQUE, MALACCA.

Cancellation: Nil
Back: Divided

Built in 1728, the Kampung Hulu Mosque's architectural style is Sumatran; it has a three-tier pyramidal roof, though its minaret has features of a Chinese pagoda. Date: c 1910

[365]
THE PORTUGUESE CHURCH OF SAINT PETER AND PAUL (350YEARSOLD.

Cancellation: 1914
Back: Divided
Publisher: Seikaido Muromachi, Tokyo

Built in 1710 by the descendants of Portuguese soldiers, the St Peter's Church is the oldest functioning Catholic Church in Malaysia. The façade is a mixture of Oriental and Occidental architecture; the interior is Iberian in style.[49]

[366]
MEAT MARKET & CHURCH. MALACCA.

Cancellation: 1925
Back: Divided
Publisher: Wilson, Malacca

The twin spires of the St Francis Xavier Church stand out prominently; in the foreground is a meat market. The riverside is on the right while Banda Kaba Road is on the left.

[367]
JONKER STREET, MALACCA.

Cancellation: Nil
Back: Divided

Many of the affluent Chinese lived in this street. Today the street is famous for its many shops selling antiques and handicrafts. Date: c 1910

[368]
Untitled [Peranakan wedding photograph].

Cancellation: 1939
Back: Divided

Photographed outside a Chinese Peranakan house, the bride and the groom are dressed to the hilt. Posing with them are two bridesmaids and a pageboy.

[369]
MALAY WOMEN, MALACCA.

Cancellation: Nil
Back: Divided

These two Malay women are observing *purdah* in their dressing; the lady on the left has simply draped her sarong over her head; she appears to be following her mistress. Date: c 1910

[370]
FISHERMEN, MALACCA.

Cancellation: Unclear
Back: Divided

As in the other Malayan states, fishermen were often Malays. This ppc shows four *sampans* returning laden with fish the fishermen have caught out at sea. Date: c 1910

[371]
WORKMAN PLOUGHING PADI (PADI FIELDS) MALACCA.

Cancellation: Nil
Back: Divided

A typical rural scene in Malacca: a Malay farmer is ploughing his rice field with the aid of a buffalo. Date: c 1930

[372]
DRINKING WATER TRANSPORT CART. MALACCA.

Cancellation: Nil
Back: Divided
Publisher: Wilson, Malacca

Prewar Malacca was often short of drinking water; those who were enterprising went around town with carts selling water. Date: c 1930

[373]
MALACCA. _ ORPHELINAT DES DAMES DE SAINT-MAUR.

Cancellation: Nil
Back: Divided
Publisher: Aulard et Cie, Paris

This sepia ppc shows the Orphanage of the Convent in Malacca. It was run by Catholic nuns who hailed from Paris, France.[54] Date: c 1910

[374]
Untitled [The British in Malacca].

Cancellation: Nil
Back: Divided
Publisher: Hakone Studio, Malacca

Here, a British man and his family are pictured in a motorcar convertible with a local driver and a servant (standing in front of the car). Date: c 1920

[375]
TAMPIN, MALACCA.

Cancellation: 1929
Back: Divided
Publisher: International Collectors Exchange, Malacca

The small town of Tampin is shown in this ppc; Tampin is 30 km from Malacca and is its nearest railway station.

[376]
MALACCA SWIMMING POOL, TANJONG BRUAS.

Cancellation: Nil
Back: Divided
Series and/or No.: 9

Tanjung Bruas, outside Malacca town, is situated by the sea; this sepia bromide ppc shows a Rest House with a swimming pool. Date: c 1930

K E D A H
S I K
KUALA MUDA
BALING
KULIM
SELAMA
KRIAN
PERAK
UPPER PERAK
PROVINCE WELLESLEY
Penang Island
George Town
Tk Bahang
Balik Pulau
Bayan Lepas
P Jerejak
Butterworth
Prai
Bagan Luar
Bukit Mertajam
Kulim
Jarak
Kapala Batas
Penaga
Simpang Ampat
S Bakap
Nibong Tebal
Bandar Bahru
Parit Buntar
Tg. Piandang
K Kurau
Alor Pongsu
Bagan Serai
Bt Merah
Reservoir
Semanggol
K Gula
Port Weld
Matang
Taiping
Pdg Rengas
Kuala Kangsar
S. Siput
Enggor
Chemor
Kati
Sauk
Chenderoh Lake
Kg Lintang
Kg Jalong
Batu Kurau
Kg. Redang Panjang
Kubu Gajah
Selama
Serdang
Terap
Mahang
Karangan
Lunas
Padang Serai
Titi Karangan
K Ketil
Tawar
Baling
Kroh
Klian Intan
Betong
Grik
Lawin
Lenggong
Temengor
Kg Tapong
Kampong Toh
Kg Tg Pari
Sik
Jeniang
Gurun
Guar Chempedak
Junun
Kobah
Tokai
Simpang Ampat
S Limau
Yen
G Jerai (Kedah Peak) 1213 (3978)
Bedong
Semiling
Tg Dawai
Kelang Bahru
Sungei Patani
Kota
Bt Prenggan 998 (3275)
G Bintang 1862 (6110)
G Inas 1801 (5909)
G Ulu Merah 1452 (4763)
G Ulu Titi Basah 1535 (5035)
Bt Ulu Laho 1203 (3948)
G Besar 1749 (5737)
G Grah 2106 (6903)
G Yong Yap
G Bubu
Sungei Muda
Sungei Ketil
Sungei Krian
Sungei Perak
Sungei Singor
Sungei Piah
Sungei Temor
FERRY

PENANG

Penang Island (PI) and its mainland hinterland Seberang Perai (formerly Province Wellesley) are often simply referred to as Penang. PI is popularly known as the "Pearl of the Orient". The Malay name is Pulau Pinang ("Island of the betelnut palm tree"). Penang is located on the northwest coast of the Malay Peninsula; it is the second-smallest state in Malaysia after Perlis.

The state capital of Penang is George Town [379; 380], while Butterworth is the main town on the mainland.

Founding of Penang

Francis Light founded a British Settlement on Penang (which belonged to Kedah) on 11 August 1786 without a treaty, deceiving the Sultan of Kedah in the process. From this inauspicious beginning, Penang, together with Malacca and Singapore, became a crown colony in 1867 and a component of the SS [377] until 1948, when it joined the Federation of Malaya. Like that of Singapore, Penang's rapid development was due in part to its geographical position at the "crossroads" of trading routes between Europe and Asia [378].

The port

Trade in Penang developed steadily following the opening of the Suez Canal in 1869. By 1872, Penang was declared a free port. In 1894, Quah Beng Kee (1872–1952), a shipping magnate, started a ferry service from PI to PW; the Swettenham Pier was built four years later.[59]

Before the Second World War, the Penang harbour was crowded with ships of every description [381; 382]. Due to their varying depths, the North [383] and South [384] Channels served larger and smaller vessels respectively. Victoria Pier [385], named after Queen Victoria, was built in 1888; passengers and goods were ferried by small boats to and from larger ocean steamships anchored further away. The Church Street Pier [386] was constructed in 1897; passengers could buy tickets from the FMS Railway Station [387] opposite the pier. A launch would then ferry them across the Channel to Prye (Prai) to board a train to Johore and Singapore.

However, the harbour was prone to silting up; the Swettenham Pier [389] was built in 1898 to overcome this problem. Weld Quay (also known as Pengkalan Weld) [388 (*upper right*); 390], built during the 1880s,[63] was named after Frederick Weld, Governor of the Straits Settlements (1880–1887). Large quantities of goods such as tin, rubber and tobacco were exported through Penang [391]; and this was the point of entry to and exit from Malaya for migrants and pilgrims [392; 393].

The hub of the colonial government

Fort Cornwallis [394 (*lower right*)] was the heart of Penang's colonial administration; it was built by Francis Light and named after Lord Cornwallis, Governor-General of Bengal. Much of the fort was rebuilt in the early 1800s; today the tall flag-post, harbour light and fortifications are prominent reminders of Penang's colonial past.

King Edward Place (Pesara Raja Edward) [399] was the location of many departments of the Straits Settlements Government.[60] At its centre is the Victoria Memorial Clock Tower [395-396; 399-400]. At Downing Street, linking Weld Quay to Beach Street, stood several government buildings [401-404]. The Police Court [405] was in Light Street facing the Esplanade, near Downing Street; it has since been renovated to house the State Assembly (Dewan Undangan Negeri). The Benet Vermont Memorial [406] was erected at Light Street opposite the Police Court; it no longer exists. At the Esplanade were the Municipal Office, Town Hall and Cricket Club [407; 408]. Near the

The sea front along Weld Quay was usually crowded with large and small vessels.
(*See* [388])

In this ppc, the walls of Fort Cornwallis (its tall flagstaff and lighthouse are in the centre) are clearly visible.
(*See* [394])

St Xavier's Institution was established in 1825 in Bishop Street before moving to its present site at Farquhar Street.
(*See* [412])

The Kapitan Keling Mosque was built in 1801 by H.A. Neubronner.
(*See* [417])

Esplanade are the Supreme Court [409] and Penang Free School [410]. The eastern half of the building was destroyed during the Japanese invasion; today it houses the Penang State Museum.

The streets of colonial Penang

The old colonial street pattern was laid out by Francis Light: Beach Street [397; 398] (east); Light Street [413] (north); Chulia Street [414] (south); and Pitt Street (west). Light assigned the various streets in the commercial area to different communities: the Malays to the south of Chulia Street; the Eurasians settled on Bishop and Church Streets and the Chinese in China and Market Streets. The Europeans occupied the north beach area.[63]

Like Malacca, Penang has a long "street of harmony"; it stretches from the Acheen Street Mosque in Acheen Street [415] to Khoo Kongsi [416] in Cannon Square, the Kapitan Keling Mosque [417 (*lower left*)] and Kuan Yin Temple [418] in Pitt Street and St George's Church [419] and Church of the Assumption [420] in Farquhar Street.

Bishop Street [421] connects Beach Street to Pitt Street; Whiteaway, Laidlaw & Co. was a department store favoured by the Europeans; the Commemorative Monument [422] was built on Bishop Street. Church Street [424] runs parallel to Light and Bishop Streets; the "Hai Kee Chan" ("Sea Remembrance Store" in Hokkien) [423], the ancestral hall and residence of Kapitan Cina Chung Keng Kwee, is on that street. The complex has since been restored and renovated as the Penang Peranakan Mansion.

The hotels

The Eastern & Oriental Hotel (E & O) [425] at Farquhar Street is Penang's most famous hotel, once described as as the "grande dame of the Pearl of the Orient".[68] The Runnymede Hotel [426] on Northam Road (Jalan Sultan Ahmad Shah) was established in the early 1900s.

The Chinese Residency at the corner of Northam and Transfer Roads was built by Cheah Tek Soon also during the early 1900s; it later became the Bellevue Hotel, the Raffles [427] and "Raffles By-The-Sea" [428]. It lies in ruins today. The mansion of Kapitan Cina Chung Thye Pin (1879–1935)[9] [429] at No. 2 Kelawai Road was transformed into the Shanghai Hotel [430] in the late 1930s; it was demolished in 1964.[8]

Sports clubs, schools and hospitals

The British introduced sports such as cricket [431] and horse-racing [432] to Penang soon after their arrival. Other social and sporting clubs included the Town Club [404], Penang Swimming Club, Golf Club and Chinese Recreation Club.

Schools in Penang included the Convent School at Light Street, and St Xavier's Institution [412 (*upper left*)]. The first Convent School in Malaya [411] was established in Penang in April 1852. Other schools in prewar Penang included St George's School [433], the Anglo-Chinese Boys' School [434] and the Government Girls' School.

Penang General Hospital [435] was built in 1906 on the site of an earlier Pauper Hospital at the junction of Hospital Road and Residency Road. A rare ppc shows The Leper Camp [436] at Pulau Jerejak.

The Kek Lok Si and Snake Temples

At Ayer Itam Village is the Kek Lok Si ("Temple of Supreme Bliss") with its famous pagoda [437–439]. Work on the temple started in 1891 but was only completed after the First World War. The pagoda is 30 metres tall and was constructed around 1930.

The Snake Temple [440] at Sungai Kluang has its origin in 1850 when a monk from China brought the image of "Chor Soo Kong", a deity known for healing the sick. One of those healed was David Brown of Glugor Estate who, in 1875, donated the land for the temple.[8]

Penang Hill and the Crag Hotel

Penang Hill (Government Hill; Great Hill) was also known as Bukit Bendera ("Flag Hill") [441; 442]. Penang Hill rises to about 762 metres above sea level; it became a popular hill resort after the construction of the funicular railway [443]; the history of the funicular railway has been described in detail by Ric Francis and Colin Ganley (2006).[62] The entrance to the Penang Hill railway [444] is near Ayer Itam.

At the top of the hill was the Crag Hotel and Sanatorium [445], once the residence of one Captain Kerr. It was sold to the Sarkies Brothers in 1905; in 1936 it was taken over by the Runnymede Hotel.[8]

Penang Hill had a post office [446] from 1902 to 1957.[64] At the highest point of the hill was the Bel Retiro, the hill resort of the Governor of the Straits Settlements. A huge cannon guarded the Bel Retiro and in front of it was flown the Union Jack.

Strawberries were once grown on the hill; hence it was also known as Strawberry Hill.

The Penang Botanic Gardens

The Penang Botanic Gardens date back to 1796, the first such gardens to be established in Malaya.[72] In 1884, N. Cantley, Superintendent of the Singapore Botanic Gardens, established the present Gardens and Charles Curtis was the first curator (1884–1903).[72] The entrance [447] is via Jalan Waterfall [448]. They are also known as the Waterfall Garden as there are several waterfalls [455],[72] as well as a reservoir and a bandstand. The flora are famous [452].

Multiracial Penang

Since its founding, Penang has had a multiracial population. Malays, Chinese and Indians formed the bulk of the population, with numerous minority races including Thais, Burmese [453], Eurasians, Arabs and Japanese co-existing harmoniously.

Four Malay women are shown in [449]; [450] shows Indian coolies and Indians with their bullock carts. The Chinese community [458] grew in numbers and importance during the 19th century; most came from South China. Descendants of immigrants who were born in Malaya are called Peranakan[52] [454; 457]. In Penang, they are referred to as the Chinese Peranakan,[53] though they mostly prefer to be referred to as Straits Chinese.

The boom of the tin industry in the 19th century and that of the rubber industry in the early 20th century made many Penangites very wealthy. The wealthy Chinese built opulent mansions [456] and furnished them luxuriously [459]. The funerals of these rich Chinese [460 (*upper right*)] were spectacular, elaborate events. The Chingay festival was unique to Penang; it took place once in nine years and the 1928 Chingay [461; 462 (*lower right*)] was the most spectacular – it was held over a period of four days.[76]

Industrial and rural Penang

Before the Second World War, tin refining (smelting) [463] and rice milling [464] were two important industries. Rice was produced in immense quantities in Penang. One of the best-known rice mills was the Khie Heng Bee Mill in Sungei Pinang.[16]

Rural Penang has long and beautiful beaches. The seashore at Kelawai[69] [465] is now the seashore of Gurney Drive (New Coast Road) after land reclamation. Tanjung Bunga (Malay for "Cape of Flowers") [466] now has several seaside hotels.

Province Wellesley

Province Wellesley (PW) was named after Colonel Wellesley (the future Duke of Wellington).[16] It is the mainland part of Penang state and is separated from the island by the narrow South Channel (3.5 kilometres at its narrowest and about 13 at its widest). The main towns in PW are Butterworth [467; 468] and Perai [469–472].

Chinese funerals were often lavish affairs. Here, the coffin is placed in an elaborate hearse and carried down the street.
(*See* [460])

The Chingay Festival was unique in Penang; it was held only once every nine years.
(*See* [462])

[377]
View of Municipal Office Penang.

Cancellation: Nil
Back: Divided
Series and/or No.: 90
Publisher: The Federal Rubber Stamp Co., Kuala Lumpur

A map of the Straits Settlements is shown (*right*). On the left is the Royal Standard; stamps of the Straits Settlements are used as decoration across the ppc. A view of the Penang Municipal Office is in the centre. Date: c 1910

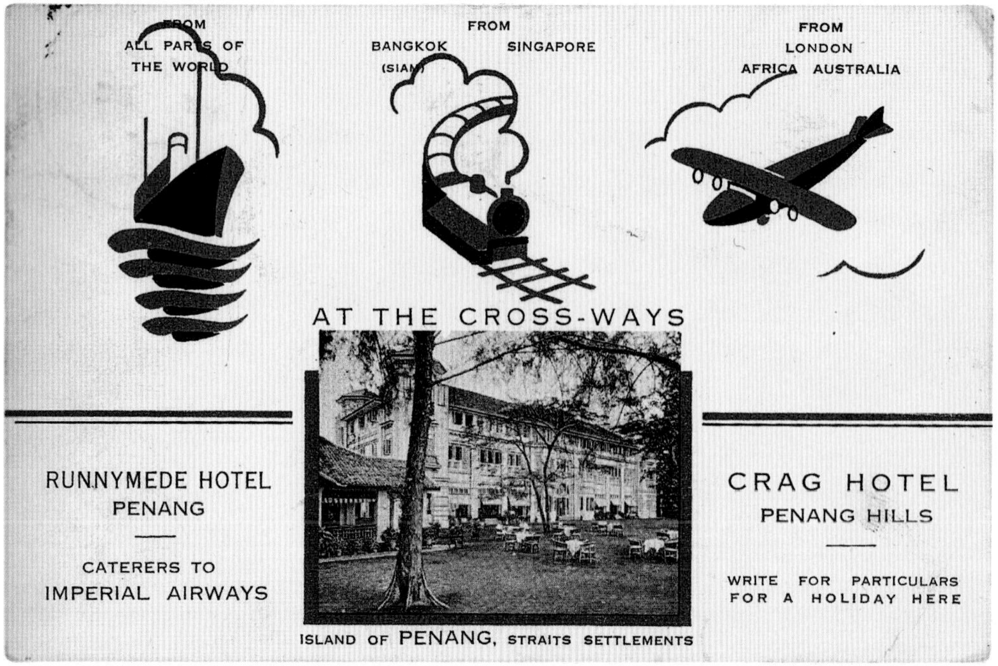

[378]
At the Cross-ways/Island of Penang, Straits Settlements.

Cancellation: 1935
Back: Divided

This ppc advertises the Runnymede Hotel (*centre*) and the Crag Hotel.

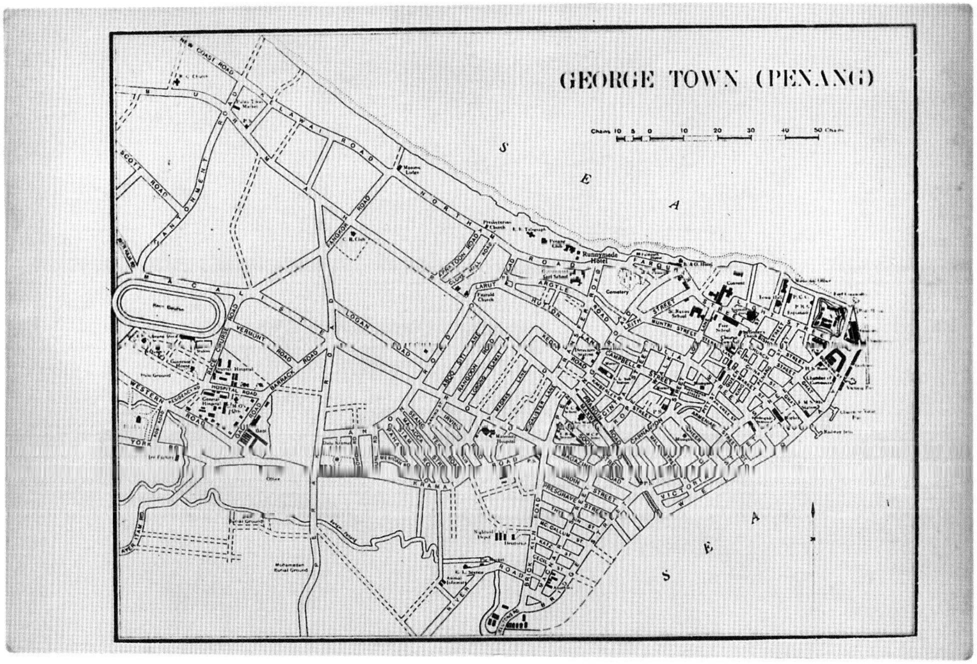

[379]
George Town (Penang).

Cancellation: Nil
Back: Divided

This unusual ppc has a map of George Town, the capital of Penang Island. George Town occupies a promontory which forms the front flipper of the tortoise-shaped Penang Island. Date: c 1930

[380]
Bird's Eye View of George Town. Penang.

Cancellation: Nil
Back: Divided
Series and/or No.: 156

This is a hand-tinted postcard of a view from Penang Hill. The promontory shape of the Town is visible. The South Channel separates the island from Kedah; in the distance is Kedah Peak. Date: c 1940

[381]
PENANG HARBOUR.

Cancellation: 1909
Back: Divided
Series and/or No.: 204
Publisher: A. Kaulfuss, Penang

This ppc depicts the Penang harbour; a *sampan* is in the foreground, with a large steamship behind it. Behind the harbour is Penang Hill.

[382]
PENANG HARBOUR. WITH CHINESE SAILING BOAT IN THE CENTRE. PENANG.

Cancellation: Nil
Back: Divided
Series and/or No.: 714

Here, the Penang harbour is crowded with larger steamships in the background and smaller vessels in the foreground. Date: c 1930

[383]
PENANG FROM NORTH.
Cancellation: 1909
Back: Divided
Series and/or No.: 97
Publisher: A. Kaulfuss, Penang

The North Channel was relatively deep and thus larger steamships entered the harbour from its north. The flag-post at Fort Cornwallis is seen on the right, and the Victoria Memorial Clock Tower is next to it.

[384]
PENANG HARBOUR (SOUTH).
Cancellation: Nil
Back: Divided
Series and/or No.: 115
Publisher: A. Kaulfuss, Penang

The South Channel was shallower than the North Channel, hence only smaller vessels entered the Penang harbour from its south. Date: c 1910

[385]
Penang. Passenger Jatty.

Cancellation: Nil
Back: Divided
Series and/or No.: 7
Publisher: Co-operative Agency, Straits Settlements

This ppc shows passengers and goods being ferried to and from the Victoria Jetty to the larger ocean steamers anchored further away.
Date: c 1910

[386]
Church Street, Pier, Penang.

Cancellation: Nil
Back: Divided

The Church Street Pier was also called the Ferry Pier. Passengers were ferried to and from the Prai FMS Railway Station. This real photographic ppc shows many vessels anchored around the pier.
Date: c 1930

[387]
CLOCK TOWER, F.M.S. RAILWAYS. PENANG.

Cancellation: Nil
Back: Divided
Series and/or No.: 136

This Railway Station never had any trains! At the station, passengers bought tickets to board the ferry at Church Street Pier and cross the Channel before boarding a FMS Railway train which would take them southwards to Johore and Singapore. Date: c 1930

[388]
BUSINESS SEA FRONT, PENANG.

Cancellation: 1937
Back: Divided
Series and/or No.: 155

In the background are the buildings that housed the European trading companies.

[389]
SWEATTENHAM PIER.

Cancellation: Nil
Back: Divided
Series and/or No.: 109
Publisher: A. Kaulfuss, Penang

The Swettenham Pier was built in 1898 for the berthing of big ocean steamers. Along the pier were railway tracks for the loading and unloading of goods. Date: c 1910

[390]
WELD QUAY, PENANG.

Cancellation: Nil
Back: Divided

Weld Quay was built in the 1880s. Many of the large European trading companies and godowns (such as Boustead & Co., Schmidt Kustermann & Co., Behn Meyer & Co. Ltd, Shiftman, Heer & Co. and Behr & Co.[9]) were located along Weld Quay. Date: 1924

[391]
SHIPPING TOBACCO BY NORDDEUTSCHER LLOYD, PENANG.

Cancellation: Nil
Back: Divided

Coastal steamers brought raw tobacco from the Dutch East Indies to Penang; it was then shipped to Europe by the steamers of Norddeutscher Lloyd (a German Company) at the Swettenham Pier. Date: c 1910

[392]
Untitled [Arrival of Immigrant Coolies, Penang].

Cancellation: Nil
Back: Divided

In this ppc; Indian migrants are disembarking at the Swettenham Pier. During the 19th to 20th centuries, thousands of migrants from India, China and the Middle East came to Malaya via Penang. Date: c 1910

[393]
Jeddah Boat, Penang.

Cancellation: Nil
Back: Divided
Series and/or No.: 38

Before the era of air travel, Muslim pilgrims from Malaya sailed by ship to Jeddah via Penang. This ppc shows a large steamship carrying pilgrims heading to Jeddah. Date: c 1910

[394]
Esplande Road, Penang.

Cancellation: 1919
Back: Divided
Series and/or No.: 3067
Publisher: K.M. Mohamed Esoof, Penang

The walls of Fort Cornwallis (its tall flagstaff and lighthouse are in the centre) are clearly visible in this ppc. The Japanese removed the iron railings on the left during the Occupation for scrap iron.

[395]
PENANG.

Cancellation: Nil
Back: Undivided
Series and/or No.: 36
Publisher: Pritchard & Co., Penang

The Victoria Memorial Clock Tower was built in 1897 to commemorate the Diamond Jubilee of Queen Victoria. This photo was taken at the official unveiling of the Clock Tower in 1902.

[396]
CLOCK TOWER AND HONGKONG-SHANGHAI BANK, BEACH STREET, PENANG.

Cancellation: Nil
Back: Divided
Series and/or No.: A43
Publisher: Nikko Studio, Penang

A view of Beach Street from the Victoria Memorial Clock Tower, taken c 1920. Below is the Hongkong and Shanghai Bank Building with its beautiful dome. This building was demolished after the Second World War.

[397]
Hongkong & Shanghai Banking Corporation. Netherlands Trading Society & Chartered Bank of India, Australia & China.

Cancellation: 1910
Back: Divided
Series and/or No.: 128
Publisher: A. Kaulfuss, Penang

The Hongkong and Shanghai Bank (building with dome) was built in 1905.

[398]
Beach Street, Penang.

Cancellation: Nil
Back: Divided
Series and/or No.: A20
Publisher: Nikko Studio, Penang

Beach Street is actually built on reclaimed land beside the beach. It was (and still is) Penang's trade and commerce hub, with many large European firms situated there. Date: c 1910

[399]
Penang. Waiting the Arrival of His Royal Highness Prince Arthur of Connaught.

Cancellation: Nil
Back: Divided

The Duke and Duchess of Connaught visited Penang in 1906; the entourage is awaiting their arrival at King Edward Place; notice the arch at the end of Beach Street.

[400]
Ditch of Fort Cornwallis – Penang.

Cancellation: 1931
Back: Divided
Series and/or No.: Sepia Postcard Series/893
Publisher: Raphael Tuck & Sons, London

This sepia ppc shows the moat (ditch) of the Fort; today the moat has been filled. The Victoria Memorial Clock Tower is visible on the left and the shorter dome next to it is that of the Hongkong and Shanghai Bank in Beach Street.

[401]
Downing Street, Penang.

Cancellation: Nil
Back: Divided

At Downing Street (named after 10 Downing Street in London) stood several buildings that housed various government departments. Date: c 1910

[402]
Downing Street, Penang.

Cancellation: Nil
Back: Divided

Among the government departments housed here were the Education Department and the Treasury. On the road, a Sikh policeman is keeping a watchful eye on the traffic. Date: c 1910

[403]
General Post Office, Penang.

Cancellation: 1920
Back: Divided
Series and/or No.: Sepia Postcard Series/893
Publisher: Raphael Tuck & Sons, London

Letters were posted from Penang as early as 1806. The General Post Office in this sepia ppc was built in 1903 but destroyed in 1941 during the Japanese Occupation.[64]

[404]
Town Club, Penang.

Cancellation: Nil
Back: Divided
Publisher: M.J., Penang

The Town Club was a colonial building located opposite the General Post Office. It is no longer in existence. It also housed the Chamber of Commerce and the Penang Turf Club. The Town Club was a meeting place for British and European businessmen. Date: c 1910

[405]
POLICE COURT. PENANG.

Cancellation: Nil
Back: Divided
Series and/or No.: 103
Publisher: A. Kaulfuss, Penang

The Police Court, along Light Street, was built in the 19th century. Today the building houses the State Assembly. It is shown here c 1910.

[406]
MEMORY OF BENET VERMONT ESPLANADE, PENANG.

Cancellation: 1911
Back: Divided
Publisher: M.J., Penang

This handsome memorial was built in memory of B. Vermont, a leading sugar planter at Batu Kawan.[8]

[407]
ESPLANADE, PENANG.

Cancellation: Nil
Back: Divided
Series and/or No.: 14
Publisher: S.M. Manicum, Penang

At the Esplanade are situated the Municipal Office (*right*), the Town Hall (*left*) and the Cricket Club (*centre*), shown here c 1910. The Cricket Club has since been demolished.

[408]
MUNICIPAL OFFICE, PENANG.

Cancellation: 1924
Back: Divided

The Municipal Office was built from 1900 to 1903; it is the most photographed building in the ppcs of prewar Penang. The front of the building consists a single-storey porte-cochère flanked by two articulated side-bays.[63]

[409]
SUPREME COURT, PENANG.

Cancellation: 1912
Back: Divided

Built in 1903, the Supreme Court is at the junction of Light Street and Pitt Street. It is a grand colonial-styled building and it was symmetrically planned to be in the form of a cross.[63] It is currently being extensively renovated.

[410]
PENANG FREE SCHOOL, PENANG.

Cancellation: Nil
Back: Divided

The Penang Free School occupied this building from 1907 to 1927 before shifting to Green Lane. At present the Penang State Museum occupies that part of the building which survived the Japanese bombing during the Second World War. In the centre foreground is the Logan Memorial (built in 1869 in memory of J.R. Logan, a prominent lawyer). Date: c 1920

[411]
Convent Garden, Penang.

Cancellation: 1907
Back: Divided
Series and/or No.: 49
Publisher: A. Kaulfuss, Penang

Being the first convent in Malaya and Singapore, the Convent Garden was established in April 1852 with an orphanage.[54] Judging from the ppc, the Convent obviously took pride in its gardens.[9]

[412]
St. Xavier's Institution, Penang.

Cancellation: Nil
Back: Divided

The Moorish building of St Xavier's Institution in this ppc was built in 1857 but was destroyed when the Japanese invaded Penang in 1941.[8]
Date: c 1910

[413]
LIGHT STREET, PENANG.

Cancellation: Nil
Back: Divided

Light Street was named after Captain Francis Light, who founded Penang in 1786. Date: c 1910

[414]
CHULIA STREET, PENANG.

Cancellation: 1914
Back: Divided
Series and/or No.: 9
Publisher: S.M. Manicum, Penang

Chulia Street was named after early Indian settlers. This ppc shows three-storey Chinese shophouses along the street, with an electric tram in the foreground.

[415]
PENANG. MALAY MOSQUE, ACHEEN STREET.

Cancellation: Nil
Back: Divided

The Acheen Street Mosque (locally known as the Malay Mosque or Masjid Melayu Lebuh Acheh) was built in 1808 with an octagonal minaret. Date: c 1910

[416]
SEH KHOO KONGSI (KHOO FAMILY HOUSE), PENANG, S.S.

Cancellation: Nil
Back: Divided
Series and/or No.: Sepia Postcard Series/768
Publisher: Raphael Tuck & Sons, London

The temple of the Khoo Kongsi in Medan Cannon was built in 1906. The architecture of the Chinese temple is magnificant; the wood and stone carvings in the temple are among the finest of its kind in Southeast Asia. Date: c 1910

[417]
MALAY MOSQUE, CHULIA STREET, PENANG.
Cancellation: Nil
Back: Divided
Series and/or No.: 3015
Publisher: K.M. Mohamed Eusof, Penang

This ppc shows the façade of the Kapitan Keling Mosque, built in 1802, facing Chulia Street. Date: 1919

[418]
CHINESE TEMPLE, PITT STREET, PENANG.
Cancellation: Nil
Back: Divided
Series and/or No.: 124

This real photographic ppc shows the Kuan Yin Temple. It is the oldest and most popular Chinese temple in Penang. The building on the right is the Chinese Town Hall. Date: c 1930

[419]
St. George's Church.

Cancellation: 1918
Back: Undivided
Series and/or No.: 38
Publisher: Pritchard & Co., Penang

Built by the East India Company, the Church was consecrated on 11 May 1819 by Rev. Thomas Middleton, Bishop of Calcutta. The domed Greek-style structure in front of the Church is dedicated to the memory of Captain Francis Light.

[420]
Souvenir of the Consecration of The Bishop of Malacca 15th April 1934.

Cancellation: Nil
Back: Divided
Publisher: Arestore, Penang

A rare photographic ppc featuring the Church of the Assumption of Farquhar Street.

[421]
JUNCTION OF BISHOP STREET, PENANG.

Cancellation: Nil
Back: Divided
Publisher: M.J., Penang

Bishop Street was so called as it was once the residence of Bishop Arnold Grasnault (leader of the Portuguese community).[8] Date: c 1910

[422]
THE COMMEMORATIVE MONUMENT TO THE ARMENIAN CHURCH, PENANG.

Cancellation: Nil
Back: Divided
Publisher: M.J., Penang

This monument stood between 1906 and 1930 at the junction of Bishop and King Streets.[65, 66] It was built over the site of the Armenian Church of St Gregory the Illuminator. Date: c 1910

[423]
Penang. Captn Ah Kevie House, Church Street.

Cancellation: Nil
Back: Divided

The caption is grossly misspelt; this was the ancestral temple cum office and residence of Kapitan Cina Chung Keng Kwee. Built in the late 19th century, it was called Hai Kee Chan (Hokkien for "Sea Remembrance Store").
Date: c 1910

[424]
Church Street, Penang.

Cancellation: 1917
Back: Divided
Series and/or No.: 36
Publisher: S.M. Manicum, Penang

Church Street was so named as it led from Beach Street to St George's Church (at the corner of Pitt and Light Streets). Many commercial offices and Chinese shophouses were located on this street.

[425]
OLD WING, EASTERN AND ORIENTAL HOTEL. PENANG.

Cancellation: 1919
Back: Divided
Series and/or No.: 13
Publisher: Waterlow & Sons Ltd, London

The Eastern and Oriental Hotel (E & O) at Farquhar Street was established in 1885 by the Armenian Sarkies brothers. With a 275 m sea frontage, it is the only hotel in the world with a sea frontage that long.

[426]
RUNNYMEDE SEA SIDE. THE ENGLISH AND CONTINENTAL HOTEL, PENANG.

Cancellation: Nil
Back: Divided
Publisher: M.J., Penang

The Runnymede Hotel was established in the early 1900s; the seafront wing shown in this ppc was built in the 1930s. It was run by two Scotsmen, Foster and Parker, until the Japanese Occupation. After the war, the hotel was converted to become the Wisma Persekutuan, the base of the Malaysian Second Army Infantry Division.[69]

[427]
RAFFLES HOTEL, PENANG.
Cancellation: Nil
Back: Divided
Publisher: M.J., Penang
This building was originally named the Chinese Residency and was built by Cheah Tek Soon in the early 1900s but later occupied by his brother, Cheah Tek Thye.[69] It was later converted to become the Bellevue Hotel and then the Raffles Hotel. Today it lies in a sad state of disrepair. Date: c 1920

[428]
RAFFLES BY-THE-SEA THE LEADING HOTEL, PENANG.
Cancellation: Nil
Back: Divided
Publisher: M.J., Penang
A printed message at the back of the ppc read: "Situated in the best part of Penang overlooking the Sea and Hills". Date: c 1930

[429]
A CHINESE RESIDENCE IN HIGH LIFE, PENANG.

Cancellation: 1912
Back: Divided
Series and/or No.: 15
Publisher: Co-operative Agency, Straits Settlements

This was the palatial mansion of Kapitan Cina Chung Thye Pin (1829–1935)[9], which extended from Kelawai Road to North Beach New Coast Road (Gurney Drive).

[430]
SHANGHAI HOTEL, PENANG.

Cancellation: Nil
Back: Divided
Publisher: The Federal Rubber Stamp Co., Kuala Lumpur

After the death of Kapitan Cina Chung Thye Pin in 1935, his mansion, shown here in c 1940, was converted to become the Shanghai Hotel. It was eventually demolished in 1964.[8]

[431]
SPORTS IN PENANG.
Cancellation: 1907
Back: Divided
Series and/or No.: 75
Publisher: A. Kaulfuss, Penang
This ppc shows a cricket match in progress at the Esplanade; the Cricket Club building is on the left.

[432]
RACES, PENANG.
Cancellation: Nil
Back: Divided
The Penang Turf Club was founded in 1864 at the site of the present St George's Girls' School at Macalister Road. In 1935, it moved to Batu Gantung.[8] Date: c 1910

[433]
ST. GEORGES SCHOOL, PENANG.

Cancellation: Nil
Back: Divided
Series and/or No.: 77
Publisher: A. Kaulfuss, Penang

St George's Girls' School (name visible in the ppc) was first established in this building in Leith Street Ghaut. The building was let out by the Presbyterian Mission.[70] Date: c 1900

[434]
ANGLO CHINESE BOY'S SCHOOL.

Cancellation: Nil
Back: Divided
Series and/or No.: 134
Publisher: A. Kaulfuss, Penang

The Anglo-Chinese Boys' School, pictured here c 1910, was built in 1896 at Maxwell Road; it moved to Pykett Avenue in 1938.[8]

[435]
GENERAL HOSPITAL, PENANG.

Cancellation: Nil
Back: Divided

The General Hospital was built in 1906 on the site of the Pauper Hospital at the junction of Hospital Road and Residency Road. Ah Poo, a Bengal-born Chinese, donated the land and built the Pauper Hospital in 1854.[8]

[436]
THE LEPER CAMP.

Cancellation: Unclear
Back: Divided

For many years (1871–1969), the Leper Camp at Pulau Jerejak (a small island just off Bayan Lepas, Penang Island) functioned as the main segregation centre for leprosy victims; its history has been well-described by A. Joshua-Raghavar.[71] Today, it is a resort island. Date: c 1930

[437]
CHINESE. TEMPLE. AYRETAE. PENANG.

Cancellation: 1928
Back: Divided
Series and/or No.: 181

This black-and-white real photographic ppc shows the pagoda (under construction at that time) of the Kek Lok Si Temple. The caption is misspelt as Ayretae; it was at the foot of the hills in Ayer Itam.

[438]
NEW PAGODA. AYER ITAM TEMPLE. PENANG.

Cancellation: Nil
Back: Divided
Series and/or No.: 179A

The Pagoda is 30 m tall. The Siamese King, Rama VII, laid the foundation stone and the Pagoda was completed around 1930. It has seven storeys and incorporates three architectural styles.
Date: c 1935

[439]
Ayer Itam Temple, Penang.

Cancellation: Nil
Back: Divided

The Kek Lok Si Temple has numerous halls housing countless Buddhist deities. On the message side of the ppc is printed: "Visitors to this Temple are always welcome". Date: c 1920

[440]
Snake Temple, Sungei Kluang, Penang.

Cancellation: Nil
Back: Divided

A number of green snakes are coiled around branches and twigs inserted in large porcelain vases and bronze urns placed on the main altar. Date: c 1930

[441]
THE FLAGSTAFF GOVERNMENT HILL.

Cancellation: 1907
Back: Undivided
Series and/or No.: 36
Publisher: Pritchard & Co., Penang

This ppc shows the flagstaff outside Bel Retiro (the rest house of the Governor of the Straits Settlements). Penang Hill was also known as Bukit Bendera (Malay for "Flag Hill").

[442]
PENANG. GOVERNMENT HILL.

Cancellation: 1908
Back: Undivided

A big cannon is guarding the Bel Retiro.

[443]
PENANG HILL RAILWAY.

Cancellation: Nil
Back: Divided

This real photographic black-and-white ppc shows a railway carriage ascending Penang Hill. Notice the service steps by the side and jungle vegetation surrounding the railway track.
Date: c 1930

[444]
ENTERANCE. P.H.R.

Cancellation: Nil
Back: Divided

The entrance to the Penang Hill Railway is near Ayer Itam. Here in this ppc, there are several motorcars parked outside the Lower Station. The funicular railway tracks leading up the hill are visible behind the station. Date: c 1930

[445]
CRAG HOTEL AND SANATORIUM ELEVATION 2260 FT./CRAG HOTEL/FOOT OF THE HILLS.

Cancellation: 1910
Back: Divided
Series and/or No.: 2
Publisher: A. Kaulfuss, Penang

In 1910, before the creation of the Penang Hill railway, visitors climbed (or were carried) up the hill. The message on the ppc reads: "Climbed up here this morning and had tiffin; came in rickshaws to foot and four of us shared chair as shown here to be carried up".

[446]
POST OFFICE, PENANG HILL.

Cancellation: 1932
Back: Divided
Series and/or No.: 7
Publisher: Penang Photo Store, Penang

Penang Hill had a post office from 1902 to 1957. The small post office building is in the centre.

[447]
ENTRANCE TO BOT. GARDENS.

Cancellation: Nil
Back: Divided
Series and/or No.: 117
Publisher: A. Kaulfuss, Penang

As one approaches the Botanic Gardens, its lush trees and flora are apparent; the entrance is still recognisable today. In the ppc, a shirtless Indian gardener is on the right and a young European man about to mount his bicycle is in the centre.
Date: c 1910

[448]
WATER FALL ROAD, PENANG.

Cancellation: Unclear
Back: Divided
Series and/or No.: 3042
Publisher: K.M. Mohamed Eusof, Penang

Jalan Waterfall leads to the Penang Botanic Gardens. On the right, enclosed by white walls, is the Naffu Kottai Chettiar Temple, which dates back to the 1850s. During Thaipusam, this road is packed with Hindu devotees carrying *kavadis*.
Date: c 1910

[449]
MALAY WOMEN – PENANG.

Cancellation: Nil
Back: Divided
Series and/or No.: A42
Publisher: Nikko Studio, Penang

Portraits of four young women taken in a photo studio; the women on the left are in traditional dresses while the women on the right are in modern *baju* and *sarung*. Date: c 1910

[450]
PENANG/BULLOCK CART/INDIAN COOLIES.

Cancellation: Nil
Back: Divided
Series and/or No.: A34
Publisher: Nikko Studio, Penang

In the top right vignette, Indian coolies are squatting and having their meals in front of several hawkers. The bottom left vignette shows two bullock carts and their Indian drivers. Date: c 1910

[451]
PRY PIER AND PRY STATION, PENANG.

Cancellation: Nil
Back: Divided
Series and/or No.: A46
Publisher: Nikko Studio, Penang

The left vignette shows passengers disembarking at Prai Pier; the right vignette shows passengers walking to the railway station. Date: c 1910

[452]
PALM HOUSE/TRAVELLER PALM/ ORCHID HOUSE/PENANG.

Cancellation: Nil
Back: Divided
Series and/or No.: A50
Publisher: Nikko Studio, Penang

The Botanic Gardens has a large number of trees, shrubs and flowering plants. Its Orchid Collection is well-known and numerous hybrids have been grown.[72] Date: c 1930

[453]
PENANG. THE BURMESE BEAUTIES.

Cancellation: Nil
Back: Divided
Publisher: T.C.B., Penang

One of the many minority races in Penang included the Burmese. Here, two Burmese women are in a studio portrait attired in typical Burmese attire. The blouses of the ladies are hand-tinted in blue and green shades. Date: c 1910

[454]
Untitled [Chinese Peranakan lady].

Cancellation: Nil
Back: Divided

This beautiful young *nonya* is captured in a formal studio portraiture. She is attired in typical Chinese Peranakan attire and is decked with jewellery from head to toe. Date: c 1930

[455]
PENANG WATERFALL/SIAMESE TEMPLE/ BOTANICAL GARDENS.

Cancellation: Nil
Back: Divided
Publisher: A. Kaulfuss, Penang

In the bottom right vignette is a view of the Gardens near the entrance. The Siamese Temple has since been rebuilt and houses a 33 m statue of the reclining Buddha. Date: c 1910

[456]
CHINESE RESIDENCY, PENANG.

Cancellation: Nil
Back: Divided

This ppc shows the mansion of a rich Chinese in Penang; it was built on a hillock with elaborately landscaped gardens. Date: c 1910

[457]
Penang Chinese Children in New Year's Dress.

Cancellation: 1908
Back: Divided

This rare ppc shows two girls and three boys dressed for the Chinese New Year. The girls are dressed in Chinese Peranakan clothing, headdress and jewellery, while the boys are attired in Manchu clothing and hats.

[458]
Chinese girls with tiny feet, Penang.

Cancellation: Nil
Back: Divided
Publisher: M.J., Penang

These girls are new migrants from South China; they had tiny bound feet. During the 19th century, they came in vast numbers to marry rich Chinese and Peranakans. Date: c 1910

[459]
INTERIOR OF A CHINESE HOUSE.

Cancellation: Nil
Back: Divided
Series and/or No.: 144
Publisher: A. Kaulfuss, Penang

Showing the reception room of a Chinese mansion; its floor is paved with tiles from England in the Victorian style. The central hanging lamp is from the Dutch East Indies and the sides of the room are lined with rows of blackwood furniture. The interior is decorated in true eclectic style! Date: c 1910

[460]
CHINESE FUNERAL, PENANG.

Cancellation: Nil
Back: Divided
Publisher: The Federal Rubber Stamp Co., Kuala Lumpur

The coffin was placed in an elaborately decorated hearse and carried by pallbearers. On the top of the hearse was a stork (indicating that the deceased was a lady). Date: c 1930

[461]
CHINESE CHINGEY PPOCESSION, PENANG.

Cancellation: Nil
Back: Divided
Publisher: Nikko Studio, Penang

The 1928 Chingay Procession in Penang was its most spectacular ever.[76] In this ppc, a long "dragon" is mounted on wheels, with young girls riding it at various sections.

[462]
Untitled [Chingay Procession, Penang].

Cancellation: 1928
Back: Divided

This ppc shows the chariot of the Goddess of Mercy ("Kuan Im Hood Chor" in Hokkien) passing through Beach Street.

[463]
TIN REFINERY/TINSLABS READY FOR SHIPPING.

Cancellation: 1910
Back: Divided
Series and/or No.: 127
Publisher: A. Kaulfuss, Penang

This ppc has two vignettes: tin smelting (*top*) and tin slabs ready for shipping (*bottom*). The violet triple-ringed "E & O Hotel/Penang" circular datestamp on this ppc is rare.

[464]
DRYING RICE.

Cancellation: Nil
Back: Divided
Series and/or No.: 136
Publisher: A. Kaulfuss, Penang

This bi-view ppc shows the process of rice drying. This ppc is most likely to be of the Khie Heng Bee Ricemill at Sungei Pinang; it was one of the largest rice mills in Penang. Date: c 1910

[465]
SEA SHORE KALAWEI.

Cancellation: 1907
Back: Divided
Series and/or No.: 52
Publisher: Co-operative Agency,
Straits Settlements

This ppc shows the seashore before the construction of Gurney Drive (New Coast Road). Before the World Wars, many Penangites referred to this area as Kelawai, and many of the rich lived here.

[466]
TANDJONG BUNGHA, PENANG.

Cancellation: Nil
Back: Divided

This ppc depicts the idyllic coastline along Tanjung Bunga (Malay for "Cape of Flowers"). Today, several international hotels dot this area. Date: c 1910

[467]
BUTTERWORTH PIER, OPPOSITE SIDE, PENANG.
Cancellation: Nil
Back: Divided
Series and/or No.: A25
Publisher: Nikko Studio, Penang

In the 1900s travellers took a small boat from Penang to land at this pier. There were a large number of Indians in Butterworth; the spire of the Sri Mahamariamman Temple is visible in the background. Date: c 1910

[468]
BUTTERWORTH, MAIN ROAD, PENANG.
Cancellation: Nil
Back: Divided
Series and/or No.: 3034
Publisher: K.M Mohamed Eusof, Penang

This town in Province Wellesley was named after William J. Butterworth, Governor of the Straits Settlements (1843–1855). The main road in this ppc is now named Jalan Bagan Luar. Date: c 1910

[469]
PRYE HARBOUR, PENANG.

Cancellation: Nil
Back: Divided
Series and/or No.: 103
Publisher: S.M. Manicum, Penang

Prye (Prai) in Malay literally means "turning right round". It is a town at the mouth of the Prai River. Here, this ppc shows the steamer SS *Perak* at the Prai Harbour transporting passengers to and from Prai and Penang. Date: c 1910

[470]
RAILWAY PRYE.

Cancellation: Nil
Back: Divided
Series and/or No.: 32
Publisher: S.M. Manicum, Penang

The railway line between Prai and Seremban in Negri Sembilan was completed in 1903; this facilitated the transport of people and goods. Here, a steam railway train is pulling out of the Prai Railway Station. Date: c 1910

[471]
RAILWAY STATION, P.W.

Cancellation: Nil
Back: Divided

This ppc shows a group of Europeans posing besides a train at the Railway Station in Prai. Date: c 1920

[472]
PRYE COAL STORE.

Cancellation: 1921
Back: Divided
Series and/or No.: 103
Publisher: S.M. Manicum, Penang

The stockyard stored the coal used to drive the engines of the trains. This ppc is rare, as the use of a mixture of Straits Settlements and FMS stamps on any ppc is uncommon.

PANORAMAS, MULTIVIEWS and BOOKLETS

A brightly coloured two-view ppc containing two views of the altars at the Kek Lok Si Temple in Ayer Itam.
(*See* [481])

A multiview ppc with four views ("Panorama of Penang Landing", "Landing Pier", "Post Office" and "Beach Str").
(*See* [489])

Panoramic picture postcards

Panoramic ppcs of Malaya are rare; only one example has ever been published.[9] Unlike Singapore panoramic ppcs which exist in two, three or four folds,[2] the Malayan panoramic ppc has only two folds. An ordinary ppc measures 14 x 9 cm (5.5 x 3.5 inches) while a two-fold panoramic ppc is twice as long (28 x 9 cm or 11.0 x 3.5 inches). Panoramic ppcs are meant to be folded when posted. However, most of the panoramic ppcs found today are unused, and they usually exist in an unfolded state. No doubt their original owners were loth to part with such beautiful ppcs! This phenomenon probably explains why used panoramic ppcs are eagerly sought after by collectors today. Ppcs [473–480] show the two-fold panoramic ppcs in the author's collection.

Multiview picture postcards

Although multiview ppcs are well-known to collectors, they have seldom been classified into specific categories. There are far fewer multiview ppcs of Malaya than of Singapore;[2] this could be attributed to the fact that G.R. Lambert produced more multiview ppcs of Singapore than of Malaya. Those that do exist are, unfortunately, less striking and colourful. For example, the multiview ppcs of Penang published by A. Kaulfuss are much duller than those of Singapore produced by G.R. Lambert.[2] Lambert is regarded as the master of multiview ppcs and photographs; most of the multiview photographs in *Twentieth Century Impressions of British Malaya* (published in 1908)[16] were his work.

A simple way to classify multiview ppcs is by counting the number of views (or vignettes) in the ppc. The main views are counted; the smaller ones are to be ignored. Some of the multiview ppcs have "diffuse" or continuous images; these are classified arbitrarily.[2] The multiview ppcs in this book have been classified as below:

(A) Multiview postcards with two views [481–485]
(B) Multiview postcards with three views [486–488]
(C) Multiview postcards with four views [489–490]
(D) Multiview postcards with six or more views [491–492]

Picture postcard booklets

Picture postcard booklets (ppcbls) are well-known to collectors; those of Singapore have been described recently,[2] but little is known of those from Malaya. Ppcbls of Malaya were issued from 1910 to 1940; they are all in black-and-white or in sepia tones. Each ppcbl usually contains 12 ppcs, but the number can vary from 6 to 20; the ppcs are usually stapled together but may also be stitched. Each ppc is detachable (usually on the left-hand side) from the spine of the ppcbl; hence such a detached ppc has a serrated left border. A ppcbl measures 15.5 x 9.4 cm (6.1 x 3.7 inches). Some ppcbls have silk paper slotted in between the cards. Ppcbls were produced from 1910 onwards, and the ppcs in them have divided backs.

Ppcbls of Singapore are commoner than those of Malaya; a few of them have a mixture of Singapore and Malaya ppcs. The ppbcls in the author's collection are:

(1) A ppcbl of six panoramic ppcs in sepia tone (*below*); ppcs from the booklet show scenes such as the "View from Police Depot" and "Railway Station, Kuala Lumpur". This ppcbl has a green cover with the imprint "Series No. 19. Six Picture Post Cards. The Federal Rubber Stamp Co., Penang, Kuala Lumpur & Ipoh". This is a rare ppcbl and was issued around 1910.

(2) The cover of this ppcbl (*right, top*) has brown wording on a grey background. The first ppc is that of the "Ayer Itam Temple, Penang" and the last ppc is "Fruit & Vegetable Vendors, Penang". It was published by The Federal Rubber Stamp Co. around 1910.

(3) This ppcbl has 12 ppcs published by The Federal Rubber Stamp Co. around 1910. The first ppc is of the "Clock Tower, Penang" and the last ppc shows the "New Harbour Light". The cover is green and it belongs to "Series No. 16".

(4) This ppcbl (with the imprint "12 Views of Singapore. Malaya. Series I" on its cover) has 11 ppcs of Singapore, with a single ppc of Malaya that depicts the Ubad Alah Mosque of Kuala Kangsar. The cover is red with black lettering; the publisher is unknown.

(4) On the cover of this ppcbl is: "Penang Views. I. 12 pictures of famous Buildings with Greetings". It was published by The Publicity & Clerical Agency, Penang, around 1940. The first ppc is of "The Municipal Office, Esplanade Road" and the last card is the "Kek Lok Si Temple, Ayer Itam".

The cover of this ppcbl is slighty greyish in colour and contains 12 "detachable post card views of Penang". This booklet was published by The Federal Rubber Stamp Co.

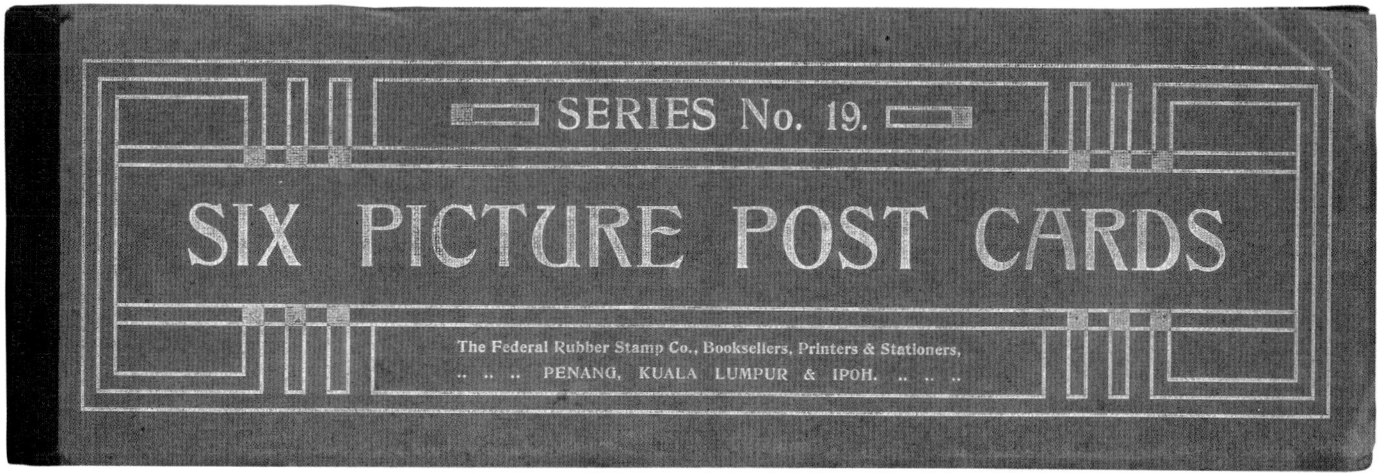

This ppcbl has a marine-green cover with silver wordings, and it contains six sepia-toned two-fold panoramic ppcs.

[473]
PANORAMA OF PENANG.

Cancellation: Unclear
Back: Divided

This is a view of George Town stretching from Kedah Pier (*right*) all the way to Weld Quay (*left*). From right to left can be seen the flag post of Fort Cornwallis; the Queen Victoria Clock Tower; the Government Buildings; the buildings of the European trading companies and Swettenham Pier, Victoria Pier, Church Street, Ghaut Pier and the Railway Jetty. Date: c 1910

[474]
PENANG. PANORAMIC VIEW.

Cancellation: Nil
Back: Divided
Series and/or No.: 35
Publisher: Co-operative Agency, Straits Settlements

This panorama is taken closer to shore than [473]. The view stretches from the Government Buildings on the right to Weld Quay on the left. Date: c 1910

[475]
SUPREME COURT AND TOWN HALL, KUALA LUMPUR, SELANGOR. F.M.S.

Cancellation: 1918
Back: Divided
Series and/or No.: 388
Publisher: The Federal Rubber Stamp Co., Kuala Lumpur

This rare panoramic ppc shows the Supreme Court and Town Hall in Kuala Lumpur; beyond it is the Bangunan Sultan Abdul Samad. All these buildings were constructed in the British "Raj" style.

[476]
VIEW FROM GOMBAK BRIDGE, KUALA LUMPUR, SELANGOR, F.M.S.

Cancellation: Nil
Back: Divided
Series and/or No.: 386
Publisher: The Federal Rubber Stamp Co., Kuala Lumpur

On the left of the ppc is the Bangunan Sultan Abdul Samad; it was built between 1894 and 1897. It is the most photographed building on ppcs of Kuala Lumpur. Opposite it is the Selangor Club; between the two buildings is the Padang. Date: c 1910

[477]
MUSEUM. KUALA LUMPUR, SELANGOR, F.M.S.
Cancellation: 1910
Back: Divided
Series and/or No.: 389
Publisher: The Federal Rubber Stamp Co., Kuala Lumpur

A panoramic view of the Museum taken from the junction between two roads. The message on the back of the ppc reads: "Just arrived Kuala Lumpur. Got to Penang tonight. Very interesting country..."

[478]
PUBLIC GARDENS, KUALA LUMPUR, SELANGOR, F.M.S.
Cancellation: 1910
Back: Divided
Series and/or No.: 387
Publisher: The Federal Rubber Stamp Co., Kuala Lumpur

A panoramic view of Lake Gardens (sometimes referred to as "Sydney Lake"), Kuala Lumpur.

[479]
THE MOSQUE, JOHORE BAHRU.
Cancellation: Nil
Back: Undivided

The sepia-toned panoramic ppc features the Sultan Abu Bakar Mosque in Johore Bahru. It was built from 1892 to 1896. To the right of the mosque is the Straits of Johore with Singapore in the horizon. Date: c 1910

[480]
THE JOHORE CAUSEWAY.
Cancellation: Nil
Back: Undivided

The Johore Causeway was opened in 1924. This is the view from the Johore end towards Singapore. Date: c 1925

[481]
CHINESE TEMPLE AYER ITAM, PENANG.

Cancellation: 1917
Back: Divided
Series and/or No.: A45
Publisher: Nikko Studio, Penang

This ppc contains two colourful views of the altars at the Kek Lok Si Temple in Ayer Itam.

[482]
THE WAY TO THE HILLS PENANG.

Cancellation: 1903
Back: Undivided
Publisher: A. Kaulfuss, Penang

The left vignette shows the entrance to Penang Hills from the Botanic Gardens, while the right vignette presents the view of Europeans being carried up the hill on Sedan chairs.

[483]
Penang, Municipal Office/Penang, Malay Village.

Cancellation: Nil
Back: Undivided
Series and/or No.: 209

The top view of this bi-view ppc is that of the Municipal Office at the Esplanade while the bottom shows a Malay village in rural Penang. Date: c 1900

[484]
Light Street/Elephants Bathing.

Cancellation: Nil
Back: Divided
Series and/or No.: 129
Publisher: A. Kaulfuss, Penang

This ppc has two views: Light Street and the Supreme Court in Penang (*top*); elephants bathing in the river (*bottom*). Date: c 1910

[485]
BEACH STREET, PENANG/GOTTLIEB TREE.

Cancellation: Nil
Back: Divided
Series and/or No.: 57
Publisher: A. Kaulfuss, Penang

A ppc with two views of Beach Street and of a "Gottlieb Tree". The Gottlieb Tree resembles a tall rain tree. Date: c 1910

[486]
PRY PIER/PRY STATION/STATION BUILDING, PENANG.

Cancellation: Nil
Back: Divided
Series and/or No.: A48
Publisher: Nikko Studio, Penang

The two smaller views at the top show the Prai Pier and Railway Station in PW; the bottom view is that of the Station Building on Penang Island. Date: c 1910

[487]
PENANG/PENANG CLUB.

Cancellation: Nil
Back: Divided
Publisher: Kleingrothe, Deli Sumatra

This rare azure-toned ppc shows a vignette of the Penang Club; it is flanked by two other vignettes showing a Chinese Mandarin and an Indian boy. Date: 1900

[488]
PENANG/HARBOUR.

Cancellation: Unclear
Back: Undivided
Publisher: Kleingrothe, Deli Sumatra

A rare tri-view ppc showing the vignettes of the Penang Harbour, a young Indian lady and an Orang Utan. This ppc is unusual in that it has a printed date (1900) alongside its left border.

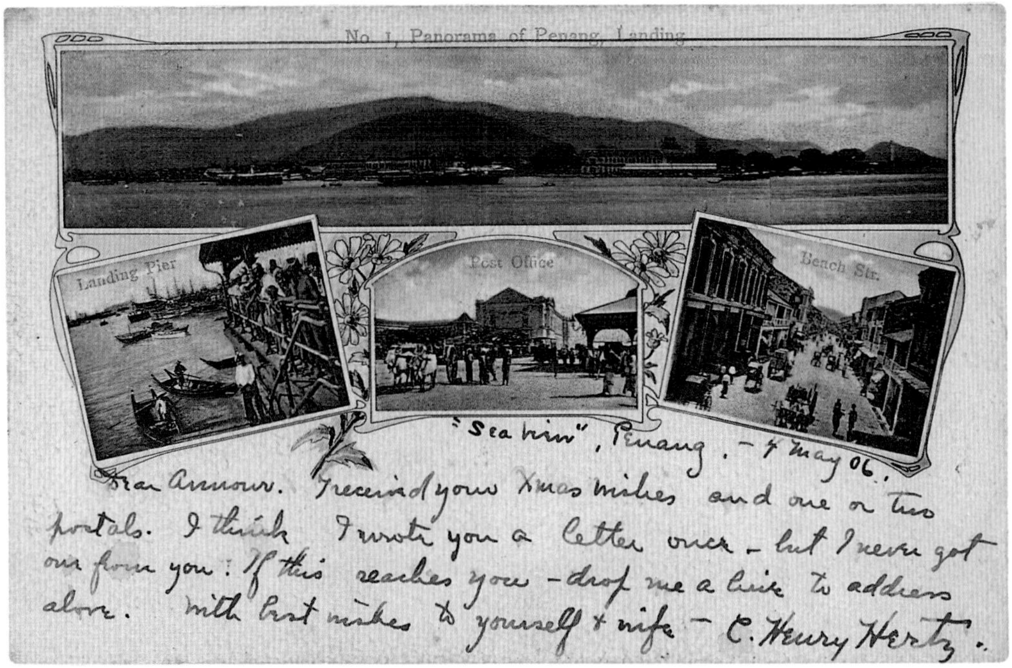

[489]
No. 1, Panorama of Penang, Landing.

Cancellation: 1906
Back: Divided
Series and/or No.: 1
Publisher: Kleingrothe, Deli Sumatra

A multiview ppc with four views; the border of the centre view is decorated with floral drawings.

[490]
Greetings from Penang.

Cancellation: 1902
Back: Divided
Series and/or No.: 4
Publisher: A. Kaulfuss, Penang

This mulitview ppc of Penang has four views, which comprise Malay ladies and a bearded Sikh man.

[491]
PENANG.

Cancellation: 1904
Back: Undivided

There are five views in this black-and-white Penang multiview ppc: a Chinese rickshaw puller; the Waterfall Gardens; Hindu women; a Hindu temple and a Malay man standing outside a house.

[492]
PENANG.

Cancellation: Nil
Back: Divided

A beautifully coloured multiview ppc. It shows vignettes of a hawker, the Penang harbour, the Waterfall Gardens, a Chinese Temple and priests. A seaside scene provides the backdrop to the vignettes. Date: c 1910

PHILATELIC ASPECTS

FMS stamps that were used in Kedah are rare, especially when the cancellation marks are clear. (*See* [495])

This ppc is franked with overprint stamps from the 1922 Malaya Borneo Exhibition. (*See* [499])

A picture postcard (ppc) has two sides: the picture side and the address/message/stamp side. Cartologists (deltiologists or cartophilists) regard the picture side of the ppc as being more important. Philatelists, however, place greater emphasis on other aspects such as the type of stamp used, the address and the message. This is because these small details can enhance the value of a ppc considerably. Hence, whenever one is buying a ppc, it is important to examine both sides of it very carefully.

The postal history of each ppc includes the type and rate of the stamp used; the cancellation date; the route taken; and the message on the ppc. In an unused (mint) ppc there is only one side to scrutinise. However, a used ppc with the cancelled stamp intact is more valuable than an unused one.

The address/message/stamp side

A well-known sender or addressee (e.g. the Governor or Sultan) increases the value of any ppc. Most of the messages printed on ppcs are of greetings and salutations; some messages "humanise" a card **[493]** while others are printed for advertising purposes **[494]**. Unusual and interesting messages also enhance the value of a ppc.

Uncommon stamps **[495–498]** or uncommon cancellations **[499; 500]** increase the value of a ppc considerably; hence it is important to examine the stamp and the cancellation closely when buying a used ppc. In Kedah, from 1909 to 1912, FMS stamps were used **[495** (*upper left*)**]** before the introduction of Kedah stamps. Similarly in Kelantan, FMS stamps **[496]** were used before the state started printing its own stamps in 1911. Prewar, Perlis produced no ppcs or stamps; it used Penang or other Malayan states' ppcs and Kedah stamps instead **[497]**.

Other examples of uncommon features on ppcs include the following: the 4¢ Straits Settlements stamp issued to commemorate the Coronation of King George VI **[498]**; a ppc of the E & O Hotel, Penang, bearing the 2¢ and 4¢ Straits Settlements stamps with the "Malaya Borneo Exhibition" overprints of 1922 (these stamps are rare on covers or ppcs) **[499** (*lower left*)**]**; and a ppc bearing a 4¢ "Sultan Ismail of Johore" stamp tied by a "British Empire Lion Exhibition 1924" date-stamp (this commemorative date-stamp on a ppc is rare) **[500]**.

Valuation

The value of an unused ppc is usually determined by how common the scene printed on its picture side is. For example, a common scene on a ppc is worth \$5–\$30, while a ppc depicting a rare scene could easily be sold for several hundred dollars.

For used ppcs, the scarcity of the postage stamp and cancellation mark determines their value. In the context of this publication, the most valuable of the Malayan ppcs would be the ones franked with Siamese stamps and tied with the short-lived Siamese postal cancellations. Such ppcs may be worth several thousand dollars.

Generally, the value of ppcs can be determined by the following factors: age, condition, colouring, rarity and usage.

Conclusion

How many different ppcs of Malaya were published from 1898 to 1941? In Penang alone, a rough estimate would be about 1500–2000. However, the exact number fluctuates from state to state; the more affluent a state was during that period of time, the larger the number of ppcs published.

[493]
Penang from the Sea. Penang.

Cancellation: 1907
Back: Undivided
Series and/or No.: 16
Publisher: Pritchard & Co., Penang

The interesting message on the back reads: "We motored here two days ago 117 miles... had a splendid ride... very pretty place but for some reasons or other the mosquitoes are very very bad. We are all badly bitten..."

[494]
Eastern and Oriental Hotel. Penang, The New Wing.

Cancellation: Nil
Back: Undivided

The message side of the ppc is an advertisement that refers to the hotel as "The Gateway to Malaya and the Far East". Date: c 1930

[495]
Penang. Botanical Garden.

Cancellation: 1910
Back: Divided
Series and/or No.: 13
Publisher: T.C.B., Penang

The picture on the ppc is common but FMS stamps used in Kedah are rare, especially when the cancellation marks are clear. This ppc is franked with three FMS 1¢ stamps and tied with the Siamese bilingual "Swiss type" cancellation.

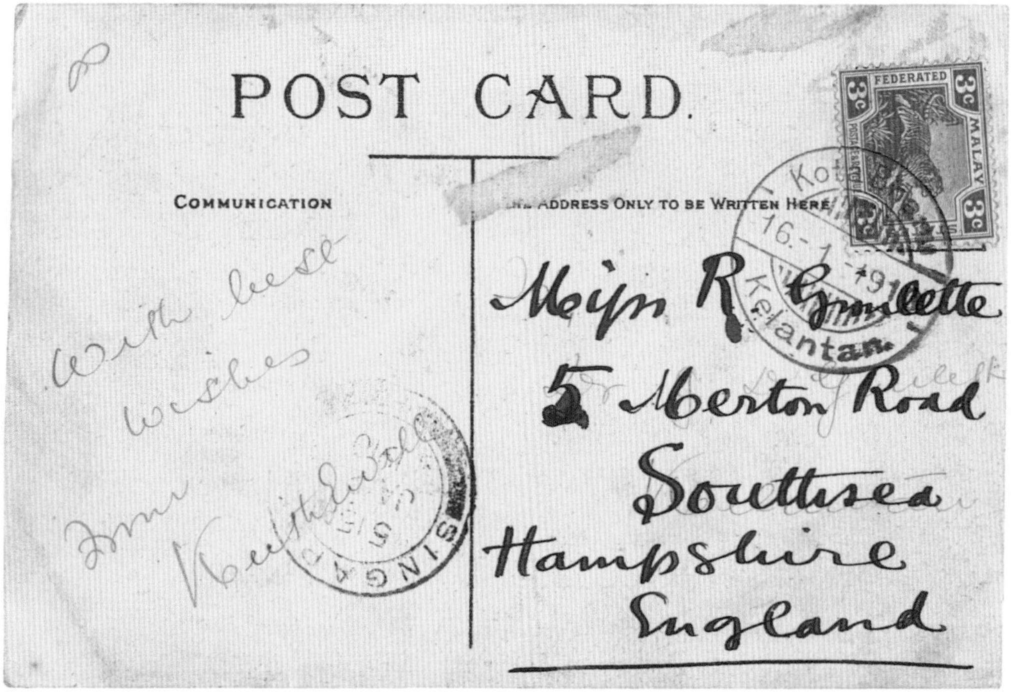

[496]
Untitled [General Hospital, Selangor].

Cancellation: 1910
Back: Divided

This rare ppc has a FMS 3¢ stamp that is tied by a cancellation mark "Kota Bahru/16-1-1910/ Kelantan" and has a Singapore transit date-stamp. It was sent from Kelantan by Dr Gimlette to his sister in England.

[497]
WATERFALL GARDEN.

Cancellation: 1934
Back: Divided

Prewar Perlis had no ppcs or stamps of its own; the sender in Kangar, Perlis, used a ppc of Penang with a Kedah stamp. Ppcs sent from Perlis using Kedah stamps are scarce.

[498]
BIRD'S EYE VIEW OF GEORGE TOWN, PENANG.

Cancellation: 1937
Back: Divided
Series and/or No.: 156

This ppc was franked with a Straits Settlements 4¢ Coronation stamp of King George VI and Queen Elizabeth; it was used on the first day of issue.

[499]
E. & O. HOTEL SEA VIEW. PENANG.

Cancellation: 1922
Back: Divided
Series and/or No.: 1
Publisher: E. & O. Hotel, Penang

This ppc is franked with Straits Settlements stamps (2¢ and 4¢) with the Malaya Borneo Exhibition overprints of 1922; these stamps are rare on ppcs or covers. The message on the back reads: "...were married this morning... had a great reception here... the sea is beautiful..."

[500]
THE MARKET JOHORE BAHRU.

Cancellation: 1924
Back: Divided

This ppc is franked with a 25¢ Sultan Ibrahim of Johore stamp; the stamp is tied with the commemorative cancellation "British Empire Lion Exhibition 1924"; this cancellation is rare on a ppc.

ACKNOWLEDGEMENTS

I would like to extend my heartfelt thanks to:

- Mr Timothy Auger, Mr Gregory Lee and the team at Editions Didier Millet for making this book possible.
- Mr Peter How Kian Huat for technical help.
- My fellow collectors for useful information: Mr Khoo Boo Chia, Mr Winson Saw, Mr Wong Kum Choon, Mr Ian Anderson and Mr Alex Teoh.
- Miss Nancy Woong for secretarial help.

ABOUT THE AUTHOR

Professor Cheah Jin Seng is the author of *Singapore: 500 Early Postcards*. He is an avid philatelist and deltiologist, and is particularly well-versed in the postal history of Singapore and Malaysia. Born in Penang, he is currently a Fellow of the Royal Philatelic Society of London and a Director of the Singapore Philatelic Museum. An ex-board member of the National Museum of Singapore, Prof. Cheah has also written and co-published extensively on the subjects of stamps and postcards in Singapore and Malaysia.

Prof. Cheah also collects Chinese Peranakan artefacts, old photographs and books pertaining to the medical and local history of Singapore, Malaysia and the Straits Settlements.

By profession, Prof. Cheah is an Emeritus Consultant, Department of Medicine, National University Hospital, and Professorial Fellow, National University of Singapore. He is also a Physician and Endocrinologist, having obtained his Bachelor of Medicine and Surgery (Honours) and a Doctorate of Medicine from the National University of Singapore. He is a Fellow of the following institutions: the Royal Australasian College of Physicians, the Royal College of Physicians, Edinburgh, and the Academy of Medicine, Singapore.

FURTHER READING

1. Haks, Leo and Steven Wachlin. *Indonesia: 500 Early Postcards*. Singapore: Editions Didier Millet, 2004.
2. Cheah Jin Seng. *Singapore: 500 Early Postcards*. Singapore: Editions Didier Millet, 2006.
3. *Illustrated Guide to British Malaya*. Singapore: Fraser & Neave, 1924.
4. Ng, David. *A Retrospect of the Country through Postcards*. Malaysia: Star Publications Bhd, 1983.
5. Ng, David. *The City and Suburbs in the Early Twentieth Century*. Penang: Georgetown Printers Sdn Bhd, 1986.
6. Ng, David. *Kuala Lumpur in Postcards, 1900–1930*. Kuala Lumpur: Penerbit Fajar Bakti Sdn Bhd, 1987.
7. Ng, David and Muzaffar D.J. Tate. *Malaya – Lifestyles/1900–1930*. Kuala Lumpur: Penerbit Fajar Bakti Sdn Bhd, 1989.
8. The Penang Museum. *Penang/Through Old Picture Postcards*. Penang: The Phoenix Press Sdn Bhd, 1986.
9. Khoo Salma Nasution and Malcolm Wade. *Penang/Postcard Collection 1899–1930s*. Penang: Janus Print & Resources, 2003.
10. National Archives of Malaysia and Singapore. *Reminiscences of the Straits Settlements through Postcards*. Singapore: KHL Printing & Co. Pte Ltd, 2005.
11. Khoo Salma Nasution. *More than merchants/A history of the German-speaking Community in Penang, 1800–1940s*. Penang: Areca Books, 2006.
12. Cheah Boon Kheng, ed. *The Encyclopedia of Malaysia/Early Modern History (1800–1940)*. Vol. 7. Kuala Lumpur: Editions Didier Millet, 2001.
13. Gullick, J.M. "An overview of Selangor history." *Heritage Asia*. 2.2. Selangor: Percetakan Solai Sdn Bhd, 2005. p. 12.
14. Hawley R. "Carcosa – An Outline of its History." *Journal of Malaysian Historical Society*. No. 24. Selangor: United Selangor Press Sdn Bhd, 1981. p. 1.
15. Lam Seng Fatt. *Insider's Kuala Lumpur*. Singapore: Times Edition, 2004.
16. Wright, Arnold and H.A. Cartwright. *Twentieth Century Impressions of British Malaya: Its History, Commerce, Industries and Resources*. London: Lloyd's Great Britain Publishing Co. Ltd, 1908.
17. Various Authors. *The Institute for Medical Research, 1900–1950*. Kuala Lumpur: The Government Press, 1950.
18. Oon, Helen. *Globetrotter. Malaysia*. Kuala Lumpur: New Holland Publishers, 2000.
19. Chen Voon Fee, ed. *The Encyclopedia of Malaysia/Architecture*. Vol. 5. Kuala Lumpur: Editions Didier Millet, 1998.
20. *Negri Sembilan – Land of Quiet Grace*. 25 Sept 2006. <http://www.about-malaysia.com/negeri_sembilan/index.htm>
21. Sheppard, Mubin. *A short history of Negri Sembilan*. Singapore: Eastern Universities Press Ltd, 1965.
22. *Pengkalan Kempas Historical Complex*. 5 Oct 2006. <http://www.abc Malaysia.com/tour_malaysia/ns_historical.htm>
23. German, Ralph Lionel. *Handbook to British Malaya*. London: Waterlow & Sons Limited, 1926.
24. *Cameron Highlands History*. 5 Oct 2006. <http://www.cameron-highland-destination.com/Cameron-highlands-history.html>
25. *A Brief History of Perak*. 10 Oct 2006. <http://www.perak.gov.my/English/history/historical_background.html>
26. Teoh, Alex. *Old Taiping*. Publisher Not Stated, 2004.
27. A. Najib Ariffin. "College that Made Leaders/Malay College, Kuala Kangsar, Perak." *Heritage Asia*. 1.3. Selangor: Percetakan Solai Sdn Bhd, 2004. p. 55.
28. Khoo Salma Nasution and Abdul-Razzaq Lubis. *Ipoh/Perak/The City That Tin Built*. Penang: Janus Print & Resources, 1999.
29. Khoo Salma Nasution and Abdur-Razzaq Lubis. *Kinta Valley/Pioneering Malaysia's Modern Development*. Penang: The Phoenix Press Sdn Bhd, 2005.
30. Liew, Jeffrey. *Welcome to Ipoh*. Taiping: Sin Boon Beng Printing Sdn Bhd, 2003.
31. Khoo Salma Nasution and Chong Fong Loon. "Panorama of Old Ipoh." *Heritage Asia*. 1.3. Selangor: Percetakan Solai Sdn Bhd, 2004. p. 38.
32. Anderson, Ian. Personal Communication. 2006.
33. Khoo Salma Nasution and Abdul-Razzaq Lubis. *Taiping/Town of Everlasting Peace*. Penang: Janus Print & Resources, 1997.
34. Harrison, Cuthbert Woodville. *An Illustrated Guide to the Federated Malay States*. London: The Malay States Information Agency, 1920.
35. *Bukit Larut Forest Reserve – Maxwell Hill*. 15 Oct 2006. <http://www.malaysia-hideaways.com/highland-maxwell-hill.html>
36. Ho Tat Min. *Generations/The Story of Batu Gajah*. Ipoh: Perak Academy, 2005.
37. *The State of Johore/Malaya*. Singapore: The Advertising and Publicity Bureau Ltd, 1939.
38. Handan Abdul Jamal. "The search for identifiable Johor Architecture." *Heritage Asia*. 2.1. Selangor: Percetakan Solai Sdn Bhd, 2004. p. 40.
39. Lancaster, Paul. "Istana Centenary." *The Straits Times Annals*. Singapore: The Straits Times Press, 1965. pp. 18–21.
40. Shanmugam, S. "The Causeway." *Heritage Asia*. 2.1. Selangor: Percetakan Solai Sdn Bhd, 2004. p. 32.
41. Lim Hui Huen. *Wong Ah Fook: Immigrant builder and entrepreneur*. Singapore: Times Editions, 2002.
42. Lim Hui Huen. "Tan Hiok Nee/Major China." *Heritage Asia*. 2.1. Selangor: Percetakan Solai Sdn Bhd, 2004. p. 34.
43. Hale, Richard. "Johore Picture Postcards with Embossed Star & Crescent, 1906–1909." *The Malayan Philatelist (UK)*. 38.2 (1997): p. 30.
44. Teh Leam Seng, Alan. Personal Communication. 2006.
45. Gimlette, John. *Malay Poisons and Charm Cures*. 2nd ed. London: J & A Churchill, 1923.
46. Graham, W.A. *Kelantan*. Glasgow: James Maclehose and Sons, 1908.
47. Khoo Kay Kim. "An overview of Terengganu History." *Heritage Asia*. 2.3. Selangor: Percetakan Solai Sdn Bhd, 2005. p. 52.
48. Locke, A. *The Tigers of Terengganu*. London: Museum Press Ltd, 1954.
49. Tan, Robert. *Historic Malacca/Pot-Pourri*. Melaka: Wah Seong Press Sdn Bhd, 1989.
50. *The Singapore & Straits Directory*. Singapore: Fraser & Neave Ltd, 1916.
51. A. Najib Ariffin. "Melaka's Street of Harmony." *Heritage Asia*. 1.1. Selangor: Percetakan Solai Sdn Bhd, 2003. p. 46.
52. Khoo Joo Ee. *Straits Chinese/A Cultural History*. Amsterdam/Kuala Lumpur: The Pepin Press, 1996.
53. Tan Chee Beng. *The Baba of Melaka*. Selangor: Pelanduk Publications Sdn Bhd, 1988.
54. Penang Convent Centenary Celebrations/1852–1952/Souvenir Programme. Penang: Georgetown Printers Ltd, 1952.
55. Hayes Hoyt, Sara. *Old Penang*. Singapore: Oxford University Press, 1991.
56. Cheah Boon Kheng. "Light on a Dark Subject." *Glimpses of Old Penang*. Ed. Malini Dias. Malaysia: Star Publications, 2002.
57. Turnball, C.M. "Penang through the Years." *Heritage Asia*. 1.2. Selangor: Percetakan Solai Sdn Bhd, 2004. p. 26.
58. de Bierre, Julie. *Penang/Through Gilded Doors*. Penang: Areca Books, 2006.
59. *Historical Personalities of Penang*. Penang: The Phoenix Press Sdn Bhd, 1986.
60. Khor, Neil. "The Trade and the Port." *Glimpses of Old Penang*. Ed. Malini Dias. Malaysia: Star Publications, 2002. p. 22.
61. Wong Kum Choon. Personal Communication. 2006.
62. Ric, Franci and Colin Ganley. *Penang Trams, Trolley Buses & Railways*. Penang: Areca Books, 2006.
63. Chin Kon Yit and Chen Voon Fee. *Penang Sketchbook*. Singapore: Archipelago Press, 2001.
64. Proud, Edward B. *The Postal History of Malaya*. Vol. 1, 2nd ed. Heathfield, East Sussex: Proud-Bailey Co. Ltd, 2000.
65. Nadia, Wright. "One of Penang's historical minorities – the Armenians." *Glimpses of Old Penang*. Ed. Malini Dias. Malaysia: Star Publications, 2002. p. 47.
66. Khoo Boo Chia. Personal Communication. 2006.
67. Loh-Lim, Lin Lee. *The Blue Mansion/The Story of Mandarin Splendour Reborn*. Penang: L'Plan Sdn Bhd, 2002.
68. Khor, Neil and Yvonne Teh. "Return to Opulence: Penang's E & O Hotel." *Heritage Asia*. 3.4. Selangor: Percetakan Solai Sdn Bhd, 2006. p. 28.
69. Khoo Su Nin. *Streets of George Town, Penang*. 3rd ed. Penang: Janus Print & Resources, 2001.
70. Parfitt, I.G.J, ed. *St George's Girls' Magazine*. 1.1. Penang: Penang Gazette Press, 1938.
71. Joshua-Raghavar, A. *Leprosy in Malaysia*. Selangor: Montfort Boys' Town Printing Department, 1983.
72. Devy, Ambiga, ed. *A Guide to the Penang Botanic Gardens*. Penang: Jutaprint, 2000.
73. Lewis, Roger Scott. "The First Census, December 1788." *Glimpses of Old Penang*. Ed. Malini Dias. Malaysia: Star Publications, 2002. p. 37.
74. Cheah Jin Seng. "Opium Addiction in Penang and Malaya (1786–1941)." *To Heal the Side/The Story of Healthcare and Doctors in Penang, 1786–2004*. Ed. H.T. Ong. Penang: Phoenix Press, 2004.
75. Saravanamuttu, M. *A Souvenir of the "Kong Teik" ceremonies of the late Mrs Phuah Hin Leong*. Penang: The Criterion Press Co. Ltd, 1932.
76. *1928 Chingay Procession Souvenir*. Penang: The Criterion Press Co. Ltd, 1928.